FAITH AS AN OPTION

Cultural Memory
in
the
Present

Hent de Vries, Editor

FAITH AS AN OPTION

Possible Futures for Christianity

Hans Joas

Translated by Alex Skinner

STANFORD UNIVERSITY PRESS

STANFORD, CALIFORNIA

Stanford University Press
Stanford, California

Faith as an Option was originally published in German in 2012 under the title
Glaube als Option © Herder Verlag GmbH

Printed in the United States of America on acid-free, archival-quality paper

Library of Congress Cataloging-in-Publication Data

Joas, Hans, 1948– author.
  [Glaube als Option. English]
  Faith as an option : possible futures for Christianity / Hans Joas ; translated by
Alex Skinner.
      pages cm — (Cultural memory in the present)
  "Originally published in German in 2012 under the title Glaube als Option."
  Includes bibliographical references and index.
    ISBN 978-0-8047-8873-1 (cloth : alk. paper)
    ISBN 978-0-8047-9277-6 (pbk. : alk. paper)
    1. Secularism. 2. Faith. 3. Church history—21st century. I. Title. II. Series:
Cultural memory in the present.
BL2747J5813 2014
270.8'3—dc23

                                                                    2014006584

ISBN 978-0-8047-9278-3 (electronic)

An easy Humanism plagues the land;
I choose to take an otherworldly stand.
—JOHN UPDIKE, *Midpoint* (1969)

Contents

Foreword

In this book I have tried to bring together some of the ideas I have developed over the past few years, the product for the most part of the many talks I have given in academic and church contexts, as well as adult education institutions. I was less concerned here than in some of my other books to rigorously pursue a single train of thought. The present work has instead been shaped by my responses to questions that have been put to me. This does not, of course, excuse me from ensuring that my answers to these questions are mutually compatible.

The book's title and subtitle indicate its basic thesis and central concern. They also allude to the two thinkers who have done most to shape my engagement with the questions dealt with here: the contemporary Canadian Catholic philosopher Charles Taylor and the great German Protestant theologian, historian of Christianity, sociologist of religion, and historical theorist Ernst Troeltsch (1865–1923).

Faith as an Option builds on the ideas presented in my earlier book *Do We Need Religion?* There the focus was on the description and analysis of religious experiences, or of all those experiences that I characterize more broadly as involving "self-transcendence," and on the problems inherent in articulating such experiences. As far as contemporary religious trends are concerned, such as an increased individualization of faith, I also sought to show that "choice," seemingly the perfect concept for describing these trends, is in fact ill-suited to the phenomena of religious experience and has gained traction largely because of the predilection for an economistic vocabulary, so widespread in the contemporary zeitgeist. The title of the present work (*Faith as an Option*) may create the impression that I have now succumbed to the zeitgeist I have just criticized. But this is not the case. As some readers will immediately notice, the concept of option is in fact a way of taking seriously the basic insights of one of the most important books published on the topic of religion over the past few years. I refer here to Charles Taylor's monumental *A Secular Age* (2007),[1] whose main accomplishment is to have studied the rise of a so-called secular option, chiefly in the eighteenth century, in light of its prehistory, enforcement and impact. The rise of this secular option entails a fundamental shift in the preconditions for faith. Ever since this shift, believers have had to justify their particular faith, such as the Christian, not just as a specific confession or with respect to other religions, but also as such, as faith per se—vis-à-vis a lack of faith that was initially legitimized as a possibility and then, as I argue in chapter 3 below, "normalized" in certain countries and milieus. Of course, the rise of the secular option should not be understood as the cause of secularization; but it does establish it as a possibility. In the first instance, then, the optionality of faith arises from the fact that it has in principle become possible not to believe, and subsequently from the conditions of religious pluralism as well. This changes nothing about the fact that the unavoidable decision to embrace either faith or nonfaith or to take up one of the various religious options is not a choice as understood by economists. The book's epigraph from John Updike makes it clear that not every use of the word "choose" implies an economic choice.

Whereas the book's main title thus alludes to Charles Taylor, its subtitle is a reference to Ernst Troeltsch. Troeltsch was also central to my 2013 book *The Sacredness of the Person: A New Genealogy of Human Rights*.[2] In that case, it was chiefly because I claimed him as a pioneer of my method of "affirmative genealogy," a specific linkage of historical reconstruction and value justification. In the present book, Troeltsch plays a central role because, like few others, rather than seeking to ensure the survival of the Christian faith through withdrawal and isolation, he made what I regard as an exemplary attempt to think it through afresh in light of the most up-to-date historical research, psychology, sociology, and other sciences. It is surely redundant to add that taking him as a role model in this way does not necessarily mean that I agree entirely with his theological doctrines; given our different confessions, it would be astonishing if I did.

Because in many ways this book came about through a process of public dialogue, by taking up ideas generated through discussions in the institutions mentioned above, I am unable to list the many organizers and interlocutors individually and can merely express my thanks in a general sense. But I would like to emphasize the tremendous role in the genesis of this book played by my time as fellow at the Berlin Institute for Advanced Study (Wissenschaftskolleg zu Berlin) during the 2005–6 academic year. I am particularly grateful to Dieter Grimm, its director at the time, and the members of the "Religion and Contingency" research group, which I convened. The group included not only Charles Taylor, who discussed his great book with us during this period, as well as completing it, but José Casanova, Ingolf Dalferth, Horst Dreier, Astrid Reuter, and Abdolkarim Soroush. I would also like to mention that Paul Michael Zulehner's invitation to give a series of lectures analyzing the contemporary era from a sociology of religion angle as visiting professor at the University of Vienna during the summer semester of 2007 went a long way to helping me systematize my ideas. In addition, much of what you will read in this book corresponds to the central thematic focus of the research group on "Religious Individualization in Historical Perspective," which has been generously supported by the German Research Foundation (Deutsche Forschungsgemeinschaft) and forms part of the Max Weber Center for Advanced Cultural and Social Studies (Max-Weber-Kolleg) at the University of Erfurt. This group, however, tackles its research topics within a much broader historical framework. I am grateful to my colleagues in the research group for intellectual stimulation of many kinds. In addition to my wife, Heidrun, I would also like to thank Bettina Hollstein, Wolfgang Knöbl, and Christian Polke, who provided critical feedback on the manuscript, and Jonas Lindner, who once again provided valuable help. The outstanding working conditions at the Freiburg Institute for Advanced Studies (FRIAS) made it much easier to complete this book, for which I am truly grateful.

But the book is dedicated to my beloved grandmother Gertraud Buckel, née Grimm (May 12, 1885—October 8, 1969), for whom nonbelievers were still exotic. Rather than being optional, faith was a self-evident and central aspect of her way of life.

Introduction: Secularization
and Intellectual Honesty

"In this day and age, to be religious is to be intellectually dishonest." It was with this declaration that one of the best-known, most internationally renowned German philosophers began his opening statement at a panel discussion on religion a few years ago, for which I had been selected as his co-debater. A poor basis for mutual understanding, I thought to myself, since it is surely one of the elementary preconditions for civilized dialogue that we refrain from immediately impugning our opposite number's honesty. But it was nothing personal. It is just that many people nowadays regard religious faith as so clearly outdated—its cognitive claims refuted by the sciences, the reality of its experiential dimension explained by psychology and neuroscience, and its social functions clearly understood—that they are unable to grasp how rational individuals can possibly be prepared to sacrifice their intellects in this way. There must, they presume, be interests at play, a lack of intellectual honesty, psychological problems, or simply a lack of intellectual consistency.

The philosopher who said this claimed that his stance, so sharply critical of religion, at least meant taking the claims of faith seriously. This, he suggested, was better than simply talking of religious worldviews in the same breath as rationally grounded secular ones and calling for dialogue between their exponents. Nothing positive, he asserted, could come from a stance based on intellectual dishonesty. This stance must be exposed, its representatives confronted with vigorous argument. We mustn't make things too easy for these obscurantists.

No wonder then that our discussion became heated—so heated that the moderator virtually had to duck as the verbal volleys flew back and forth. The event continued way past its allotted time. Surprisingly, however, my sense that the audience thought our debate a disgrace and the panel discussion a failure proved to be quite wrong. I have rarely heard such prolonged applause. The very fact that we pulled no punches captivated the audience. Among both believers and nonbelievers, the intellectual justifiability of religious faith in today's world is a hotter topic than it has been for decades.

Why is this? We might mention many reasons for the rapid increase in public interest in the topic of religion—from the motives of Islamist terrorists through the issue of Turkish membership of the EU to the debate over whether religion is a significant obstacle to the integration of certain immigrant groups. All of this has been discussed so often that I shall refrain from repeating it here.[1] Of course, the parameters of these discussions are prone to constant and sudden shifts. The unanticipated mass rebellions in Tunisia, Egypt, and other Arab countries have been food for thought for all those who, until recently, declared Islam to be an obstacle to democracy. On a deeper level, regardless of these basically political issues, two apparent certainties that have undergirded arguments about religion since the eighteenth century have emerged as untenable. To paraphrase the opening statement about faith and intellectual honesty, those who ignore these shifts exclude themselves from serious contemporary debate and are merely fighting old battles.

The apparent certainty that long underpinned believers' views, the one they must now abandon, is that human beings are anthropologically primed for religion, and that if this need goes unfulfilled, whether as a result of coercion, human hubris, or shallow consumerism, moral decay is bound to ensue. As yet, the moral decline repeatedly predicted both by serious theologians and straightforward apologists for religion—since without God everything is presumed permissible—has certainly not occurred even in the most secularized of societies. The empirical connections between religiosity and morality seem to be less simple than some would like to assume.

If believers must now give up a supposed certainty, this also applies to those nonbelievers and critics of religion who see religion as past its historical sell-by date. In the eighteenth century, there emerged the idea, which would previously have been considered outrageous, that Christianity was merely a temporary phenomenon and might yet vanish from the earth. The French Revolution included the greatest state-promoted attack on Christianity in Europe since antiquity. In the second half of the nineteenth century, the notion that Christianity and religion in general would disappear without much resistance, even without the efforts of militant atheists, became so widespread among intellectuals that many felt no need to go to great pains to justify it. Modernization seemed to lead automatically to secularization—not just in the sense of the relative independence of the public sphere from specific religious precepts, but in that of a complete loss of religion. At times, even believers thought this idea plausible. This inevitably made them feel like members of an endangered species and led to the idea that the best way they could serve their faith was by resisting modernization in all its forms.

But this assumption, which may be described in shorthand as "secularization theory," or, better, "the secularization thesis," is wrong. To put it more cautiously, most experts now consider it wrong, whereas most of them long considered it correct. The hegemony within the debate has now shifted towards those who believe that there is no automatic connection between modernization and secularization, and who are looking for alternative models to depict religious change. Overcoming the thesis of secularization does not, of course, mean ignoring secularization, but rather seeing it in all its diversity. Precisely because the pseudo-explanation that modernization as such suppresses religion has bitten the dust, we must turn our attention to those cases in which religion has come under pressure or simply run out of steam.

The crucial shift of perspective here is not so much the result of new scholarly insights as of a change in the world itself. More than ever before, economic and scientific-technological modernization has penetrated societies and cultures outside of Europe and North America, in many of which Christianity is not the dominant religious tradition. But in these places the European connection between modernization and secularization is not generally being repeated. Suddenly, it is no longer the United States but secularized Europe that requires explanation as a "special case."

For demographic reasons alone, our world is becoming increasingly religious. Even the remaining advocates of the secularization thesis admit as much. The critics of colonialism were wrong in their expectation that Christianity would be viewed as a foreign implant with no future in former colonies following the end of colonial rule. In Africa, in particular, Christianity and Islam are currently undergoing enormous expansion. In South Korea, rapid modernization and advancing Christianization have coincided.

This can, of course, be evaluated in very different ways. But that is exactly the point. A historical tendency derived from the facts can no longer be used as an argument against religious faith. Both the sense of nonbelievers being at the cutting edge of progress and, conversely, the holier-than-thou self-certainty of being a morally better human being simply by virtue of being a believer have been lost.

The departure of these two mirror-image certainties is no bad thing. Believers and nonbelievers will find it easier to have a dialogue without these assumptions in the background. This may arouse interest in what the representatives of the other party are actually trying to express—through their faith or in their criticisms of a particular religion or of all religions. Curiosity about the other and a willingness to learn can thus become part of the dialogue on religion. The detritus left over from the struggles of the nineteenth century can finally be cleared away.

In political terms, this means that believers and nonbelievers will have to live with and accept one another into the future. The re-evangelization of Europe to which Pope John Paul II aspired will not bring back a unified Christian culture with political backing, no matter how spectacularly successful. Conversely, even if the proportion of believers continues to fall, even in Europe, they will remain a significant part of the population that cannot simply be ascribed to a single party or political camp. Under these circumstances, the democratic state must adopt a productive stance towards this diversity, as should all political actors. The state, Charles Taylor asserts, "can be neither Christian nor Muslim nor Jewish; but by the same token it should also be neither Marxist, nor Kantian, nor Utilitarian."[2] All beliefs may be aired in public debate; none should be viewed from the outset as superior to any other, and that includes a "reason" sharply distinguished from faith.

If we want intellectual honesty in debates on religion and secularization, then it seems to me that mutual recognition of this diversity is the key imperative.

And this has brought us to the book's ultimate destination. The first two chapters take a closer look at whether modernization necessarily leads to secularization, and whether secularization inevitably produces moral decline. The third chapter outlines an explanation of actual processes of secularization as an alternative to the so-called theory of secularization. This outline should already clarify how unsatisfactory the terms "modernity" and "modernization" are in attempting to understand the present-day religious situation. Often these terms are merely fighting words that smuggle in normative content—such as secularization—in order to then assert that what one is fighting against is past its historical expiry date. Religious movements that currently exist, and may even be gaining strength, can then be labeled mere leftovers of times past, if not a dangerous relapse that risks the progress achieved.

It is important to ask where this intellectual schema itself comes from and how it is bound up, not just with secularist, but also with specifically religious presuppositions. In chapter 4, I develop the beginnings of an answer, and show how a specific understanding of Protestantism (and not Protestant Christianity as such) developed out of a view of the Reformation and its effects as *progress*, an intellectual structure that had major consequences for ideas about modernization.

There is only one way out of the often unnoticed constraints inherent in the vocabulary of "modernization," namely, an alternative description of the processes of social change based on a greater awareness of their contingency. To this end, chapters 5 and 6, but particularly the former, seek to bring out the variable relationship between the different dimensions of modernization, which are supposedly closely linked with one another. Further, in these two chapters I discuss the possible and observable consequences of the proliferation of action options for the orientation of individuals, including in the field of religion. The proliferation of options is, of course, often considered one of the causes of secularization.

These two chapters demonstrate that, beyond the immediate concerns of this book, I envisage certain fundamental revisions of social scientific theories of social change. But this book is clearly not the right place to elaborate these revisions.[3] I believe these chapters are nonetheless vital at this point, since this is the only way to avoid squeezing signs of religious revitalization, or perhaps just an increased public attention to religion, into the schema of a "return"—of religion, of gods, of the sacred—or falsely asserting that an epochal change has occurred, as implied in the phrase "post-secular society."

Chapters 7 and 8 then turn to two issues with which we are inevitably faced in the present-day public discussion of religion: the opportunities and problems associated with interreligious communication and the supposed or real violence-inducing role of religious beliefs. Chapters 9 and 10 then examine the future of Christianity (not of *all* religions). This is done initially in a sociological vein, in other words, with respect to predictable developmental trends, and then in the sense of the identification, not bound to a particular academic discipline, of the intellectual challenges with which any Christianity that aims to be on a par with contemporary intellectual schools finds itself confronted. The process of coming to terms with Troeltsch's work, which I have been doing for years, I hope creatively, has exercised a major influence not only on this chapter but also on the assessment of "atheistic ethics" and the "cultural significance of Protestantism" in other chapters.

Is this book a religious apologia? In my opinion the description is unjustified, although it is likely that dogmatic secularists will claim precisely that. As the chapters of this book show, I would never defend religion as such, because there is no such thing as religion as such. No uniform value judgment is possible about the diverse range of phenomena covered by the term. There are only specific religions, and even these can scarcely be understood as timeless entities; they are alive in the various historically situated convictions and actions of individual believers and religious communities. Only from the perspective of secularism or in the case of a "completely amorphous yearning for religion"[4] that shies away from every concrete instance of faith does religion appear as something about which an undifferentiated judgment might be possible. But neither do I intend an apologia for any particular form of Christianity, or to reject criticisms of religion in any sweeping way. My intention is better described as an attempt to help open up a space for dialogue in which both specific religious and specific secularist assumptions can not only be articulated and related to one another but also questioned. After all, there are also such things as apologias for secularism; secularists sometimes misunderstand themselves, and on this basis, secularist presuppositions often pose as an unprejudiced attitude or as a purely rational justification. Only by opening up a new space for dialogue in this way can we provide individuals with the freedom to decide in favor of the secular option or the option of faith—of a particular faith.

1

Does Modernization Lead
to Secularization?

For a long time, most observers would have answered the question that informs this first chapter unhesitatingly and openly in the affirmative. At least since the second half of the nineteenth century, but to some extent even since the eighteenth century, and with particular self-assurance from the 1960s onwards, those who assumed that secularization was a virtually inevitable outcome of modernization enjoyed hegemonic status in every debate on religion and the future of modern society, whether in philosophy, the humanities and social sciences, or intellectual life in general. For nonbelievers, this assumption meant that they themselves stood at the pinnacle of world historical progress. They subdivided into those prepared to wait patiently for the disappearance of religion and more militant opponents of religion who were determined to speed up this process through state pressure and intellectual attacks. Both could enjoy the feeling, not of having lost something, but of having rid themselves of something that could only be an obstacle to progress, which everyone would ultimately abandon. Even believers, including theologians and church people, sometimes came to believe that modernization must go hand in hand with secularization. Inevitably, they perceived themselves as members of a species nearing extinction. If they were unwilling to give up all hope, they had little choice but to declare war on modernization itself in an attempt to delay or reverse it. A few believers here and there, unwilling to be pulled along in the slipstream of "anti-modern" political movements, saw secularization as an opportunity to purify Christianity, and thus as a divinely ordained challenge.

Of course, there were always those who resisted this hugely popular thesis of secularization. Hegemony, it goes without saying, does not mean universal validity or universal consent, but rather supremacy in the battle of ideas. Those expressing doubts about the hegemonic view tend to have a hard time of it; their views are laughed off as outmoded or dismissed as oddities. Over the past twenty years or so, however, things have changed radically. At present, at least in the social sciences, but increasingly among the general public as well, it is the doubters who have gained the upper hand, in other words those who, while they do not dispute the phenomenon of secularization, do take issue with the idea that it has a virtually law-like connection with modernization. Even under the hegemony of the doubters, of course, there are those who take an opposing view, but today the advocates of the formerly so dominant secularization thesis are increasingly on the defensive. How did this happen? Is it no more than a fashion that will die away as quickly as it emerged, or a symptom of crisis afflicting those incapable of dealing rationally with the difficulties of contemporary life? Hackneyed ideas such as these will get us nowhere. What we need to do is look more closely at the factors that substantiate or contradict the secularization thesis or appear to do so.

The meaning of the term "secularization"

In seeking to look more closely at the factors substantiating or contradicting the secularization thesis, however, we quickly come up against the ambiguity of the terms used by its exponents. Neither "secularization" nor "modernization" is a clear-cut or uncontested term. So what we need to do first is clarify what these terms are, and are not, going to mean for us here.

A number of instructive accounts have already explored the history of the term "secularization."[1] It was originally a legal term that referred exclusively to the transformation of members of religious orders into "secular priests." Studies of the concept's history have shown that this quite marginal term gained wide currency only at the beginning of the nineteenth century, when most church property became state property, or, in any case, the church lost its property, as a result of the French Revolution and the Napoleonic Wars. This process of "secularization" was soon followed by the philosophical-theological use of the term. The associated debates were concerned chiefly with "genealogical" links between characteristic features of modern society and culture, on the one hand, and the Christian faith, or religion as a whole, on the other. Key thinkers evaluated these developments in quite different ways. Certain Protestant theologians concluded that the emerging modernity was such a thoroughgoing realization of Christian ideals that the church as an institution separate from state and society would become increasingly superfluous. Others (on the radical Left) believed that those aspects of their era that they perceived as alarming resulted from a failure fully to overcome Christian thought. An as yet incomplete process of secularization must at last be brought to its radical conclusion.

This is not the place to look at these varied threads of conceptual history in detail. But they form the background to the modern social sciences, which emerged in the late nineteenth century, and the way they used the term "secularization." If the term was already ambiguous, it became even more so in the hands of social scientists. In our day, it is the Spanish-American sociologist of religion José Casanova who has made the most helpful attempt to clarify things.[2] According to him, the term "secularization" as used in the social sciences has three meanings: the generally decreasing importance of religion, the retreat of religion from the public sphere, and the freeing of societal subspheres (such as economy, science, art, or politics) from direct religious control. Countless misunderstandings have arisen because these meanings blur into one another or because those engaged in dialogue have different things in mind when they use the same word. Furthermore, the concept of "religion," which is, of course, an inherent component of every variant of the term "secularization," is anything but clear-cut, and it is very difficult to measure religious phenomena. So conceptual clarification is no more than a small step forward. In itself it tells us nothing about causal connections, such as those between the processes distinguished by Casanova. If, as in this chapter, we take secularization exclusively to mean the decreasing importance of religion, it may still refer to a wide variety of things: decreasing membership of churches and religious communities, declining participation in religious rituals, or a decreasing number of people who approve of certain religious beliefs. A general decrease in one area does not necessarily go hand in hand with a decrease in another: you can be a believer without regularly attending church services and you can be a nominal member of a church despite having lost your faith.

The notion of the retreat of religion from the public sphere is also far from unambiguous. Until striking cases of religion's public impact disabused them of the idea, sociologists of religion such as Thomas Luckmann long asserted that there was an epoch-making modern tendency towards the "privatization" of religion.[3] Others espouse the old social democratic dictum that religion is a private matter, as if it were enshrined in the constitution. What few have asked is what exactly this private sphere consists of, whether the aim should be merely to avoid close ties between church and state, whether religion ought to be absent from political life as such, or even from all public communication—and where this retreat of religion should end. In communication within families and small groups? Or perhaps even in the inner life of individuals?

Unfortunately, the second term of importance to the thesis of secularization, that of modernization, is also ambiguous. This is a topic I shall be returning to repeatedly and in more detail in later chapters of this book. At this juncture I merely wish to emphasize one particular ambiguity. Some authors refer to modernization quite innocently as a matter of economic growth and scientific-technological improvements. If we do this, then modernization has occurred in every historical period—to varying degrees, certainly, but not just in recent times. Others, meanwhile, refer to modernization in a more sophisticated sense as a process of transition to something historically new, an era they call "modernity." I reject this sophisticated variant, however, and shall restrict myself to the more "innocent" concept of modernization, for reasons explained later.[4] So with an untypical degree of conceptual clarity, the question for this chapter is: do economic growth and scientific-technological progress cause religion to decline in importance? To be precise, the question is whether these developments not only have this effect now and then, but *of necessity*, and, to be even more precise, whether this means that the decline of religion is irreversible and is not merely a historical phase or cycle. In other words, what I am concerned with here is the idea that modernization, as defined above, will eventually cause religion to vanish.

The origin of the secularization thesis

Before getting down to examining this idea, it is worth reflecting briefly on the genesis and history of this so-called secularization thesis. Since when has it existed, who supported it and how was it originally justified?

As yet, the emergence of the secularization thesis has not been thoroughly researched.[5] According to our present state of knowledge, it appears that this assumption first emerged around the beginning of the eighteenth century, but it is difficult to decide how much of this we should ascribe to improved conditions of publication and how much to intellectual shifts. The English theologian and freethinker Thomas Woolston (1670–1733), who, unable to pay the fine imposed on him because of his attacks on the clergy, died in the debtors' jail, is identified as one of the first exponents of the idea that Christianity had a limited future and would be gone by 1900.[6] In Lawrence Sterne's novel *Tristram Shandy* (1759–67), there is even a suggestion that Christianity may have ceased to exist within fifty years. At least for Sterne, however, the end of Christianity did not mean the end of all religions. Quite the opposite: he expected that it would mean the reemergence of "every other heathen god and goddess," with Jupiter at their head and Priapus at the end of their procession.[7] Predictions of Christianity's disappearance were common in the continental Enlightenment; Friedrich II of Prussia, for example, saw the idea of the decline and disappearance of a now untenable faith as showing the shape of things to come.[8] A famous example from North America is to be found in an oft-cited letter by Thomas Jefferson from 1822, in which he reduces the teachings of Christianity to a clear and simple moral doctrine provided by Jesus and joyfully declares that in the land of the free, where neither kings nor priests exercise control over faith and conscience, every young man currently alive will have become a "Unitarian" by the end of his life.[9]

In the nineteenth century, these scattered developments came together to form a broad stream. By the end of the century at the latest, almost everybody who was anybody in philosophy, the humanities, and the social sciences supported the thesis of secularization. It is not surprising that Marxists, who were largely excluded from academic life, espoused this notion. But even the greatest thinkers and scientists of the time, such as Max Weber and Emile Durkheim, Sigmund Freud, and

George Herbert Mead, not to mention Friedrich Nietzsche, one of the most vehement critics of Christianity, believed, in one form or another, in the inevitable advance of secularization. Of course, we can debate what exactly the assumption of secularization meant to each of these complex thinkers. Max Weber's term "disenchantment" cannot be simply equated with "secularization"; he was essentially concerned with the "demagification" of religion, but saw a personal striving for salvation as inevitable. Emile Durkheim's research made him aware of the dynamics of repeated processes of sacralization, including that of secular entities—the "nation" in the case of nationalism, the "person" in the case of human rights. Also important, of course, are the connections between the thesis of secularization and the cultural struggles of the nineteenth century. All these authors participated in these struggles, which informed their work, and they already interpreted them in light of theories of secularization.[10] The exponents of the secularization thesis are so numerous that we must go out of our way to find exceptions. But they certainly exist. The most significant are probably Alexis de Tocqueville, William James, Jacob Burckhardt, Ernst Troeltsch, and Max Scheler, and we can profitably draw on the work of all these authors today. After World War II, and especially in the 1960s, the thesis of secularization seemed even more self-evident. In 1968, the noted Protestant sociologist of religion Peter Berger predicted in the *New York Times* that by the year 2000, there would be virtually no religious institutions left, just a few believers here and there, isolated pockets in a sea of secularity.[11] The most important dissenting voice during this period was that of the English sociologist of religion David Martin, who expanded his initially timid objections into an impressive, historically profound, and increasingly global research program, which now amounts to a political sociology of religion.[12]

But how did the many exponents of the secularization thesis justify their assumptions? An initial response might be that they didn't much bother. For many, it all seemed so obvious that they felt little need to carefully examine the theoretical underpinnings of their views or empirical evidence. This is why I prefer to talk of the *thesis* rather than the *theory* of secularization. As far as theoretical justifications are concerned, the underlying understanding of religious faith is obviously crucial. This understanding may seem justified to a given thinker but may appear far more problematic to believers or those more schooled in matters of faith.

We most often find three types of understanding of religion in the relevant texts. Religious faith may be understood in an essentially cognitive sense as immature or insecure knowledge, as pseudoscience or a misguided attempt to solve cognitive problems. Religious faith may also be understood as an expression of hardship—material want, social and political repression, the unbearable meaninglessness of cruel twists of fate, or existential insecurity. The best-known example here is probably Marx's reference, in the introduction to his critique of the Hegelian philosophy of right, to religion as the "sigh of the oppressed creature" and the "opium of the people."[13] Religious faith may still be understood as dependent on conditions under which no doubts arise or doubts are suppressed by authorities. In many cases, the three types are linked or fused together. In desperate circumstances, some believe, people develop compensatory fantasies that limit their capacity for independent critical thought, or ruling powers exploit the situation, deploying religions to anaesthetize the public.

All three types suggest that modernization can be expected to weaken religion. This is very clear in the case of the first, "cognitive" type. If faith is immature and insecure knowledge, then over the long term it will be ill-equipped to withstand the advance of science. It will be replaced by a superior, secure form of knowledge; the mysteries of religion will be revealed to consist in psychological mechanisms (Freud) or social dynamics (Durkheim); rituals will be replaced by a "linguistification of the sacred" (Habermas). If the accent is on the idea of religion as compensation for experiences of lack, repression, or existential insecurity, then it is thought that increasing prosperity, improved opportunities for political participation and increased life expectancy are bound to suppress religion. Finally, if we believe that cultural homogeneity and authoritarian education are necessary conditions for the transmission of faith, then growing cultural pluralism, individualization and democratization of educational methods must be causal factors in the weakening of religion. These assumptions, which I have kept separate here, may also be fused together to create models of mutually reinforcing forces of secularization.

Yet all of these interpretations of religious faith are questionable at their point of departure. Faith, I would suggest, should be understood in light of the phenomenon of trust-forming rather than acquisition of knowledge, in light of experiences of certainty in the context of both suffering and joy, as providing insights into the conditions of individual autonomy rather than just the restriction of this autonomy. In any case, predictions about religious change stand on an extremely shaky foundation if the understanding of religious faith inherent in them is inadequate. Evaluating the thesis of secularization thus requires us to appropriately analyze the dynamics of religious experience and their interpretation. I can do no more here than refer to these projects, which I have pursued in other writings.[14]

A sociological examination of the secularization thesis

I am not concerned here to engage in a fundamental debate about faith but to consider the social reality of faith, in other words to evaluate the secularization thesis sociologically. If we begin by meeting the exponents of this thesis halfway and assuming that it is empirically plausible that large parts of Europe are characterized by a law-like connection between modernization and secularization, we must then examine four issues: (1) whether the European "exceptions" to the rule of secularization can be explained satisfactorily by secularization theory; (2) the precise nature of the great "exception" of the United States; (3) the picture that emerges from a non-Eurocentric perspective; and (4) how older European religious history appears in secularization theory. I can, of course, examine these points only briefly here.

1. Undisputed exceptions to the secularization of Europe are countries such as Poland and Ireland, but also Croatia to some extent and for a long time Old Bavaria (Altbayern). Exponents of secularization theory explain the relative resilience of religion in these countries or regions by pointing to the fusion of religious and national identity. For the Poles, Catholicism was undoubtedly always the central plank of their resistance to the Protestant Prussians and the Orthodox or Communist Russians,

and much the same can be said about the Catholic Irish in their resistance to the Protestant British. In no way do I dispute that such a connection exists; but I dispute the idea that because of this, we should conceive of religion as a mere relic that continues to exist for political reasons, but should really have been wiped out by modernization. This perspective disguises the fact that religious identity often became clearly distinguished only through the same process as national identity, or was at least strengthened and spread, and perhaps instrumentalized, through this process. The political mobilization of religion may involve a process of retraditionalization. Here forms of religious practice that were on the way out undergo a revival or may even be reinvented as pseudo-traditions. Such political mobilization entails new risks of religious exclusion. If national and confessional identity are closely related, then following the achievement of national independence, it is difficult for a confessional minority not to be identified with the old repressive power. This applied, for example, to Protestants in independent Ireland. As the conflict in Northern Ireland shows, such conflicts continue to exist in contemporary Western Europe. In terms of present-day global politics, however, the political mobilization of Islam is of incomparably greater significance than that of the various Christian confessions. Again, it is quite false simply to regard Islam as a traditional relic in the modern world. Much the same applies to the political mobilization of Hinduism in India or of Buddhism in Sri Lanka. If we wish to gain an adequate understanding of these phenomena, it is crucial to liberate ourselves from the notion of religion as a relic and take seriously the contemporary creative power of religious motives.

2. In the case of the European exceptions, it has always been possible to classify the less secularized societies as less modern, but this is impossible in the case of the United States. No one seriously disputes the "modernity" of the United States. And no one disputes that, according to every indicator—however contested these may be in the detail—the United States exhibits substantially and continuously higher values for religiosity than almost any European society.[15] The United States is religiously vibrant and even productive: new forms of propagation have emerged there (televangelism, megachurches) along with a ceaseless flow of often successful new religious movements (Mormonism, Pentecostalism). We can even identify significant precursors of the internal self-reform of

the Catholic Church through the Second Vatican Council there. Today, the United States leads the way in the reception of East Asian religiosity among educated Westerners, and it is more generally the setting for a process of mutual influence among all existing religions that is probably more intensive than anywhere else in the world.

In empirical terms, the long popular assumption that we can explain this case, like the European "exceptions," with reference to the fusion of national and religious identity (such as the Puritan legacy of the United States), collapsed when studies found that between 1800 and 1950, the membership of religious communities in the United States grew continuously and roughly trebled (relative to the population).[16] There is thus no question of this merely being a case of delayed secularization.

Another obvious explanation is also empirically untenable. We might think that America's religiosity, although not a legacy of the Puritan Pilgrim Fathers, is something that later generations of immigrants brought along with them. Since many of them came from Poland and Ireland, this would make the American case a kind of geographical displacement of European backwardness or anomalies. But studies have shown that immigrants usually became more religiously active as a result of their migration to the United States than they were before. This still applies (with a few exceptions) to present-day migration.

The explanation that currently seems most persuasive derives the religious vitality of the United States from the religious pluralism associated with an early separation of state and "church," although this is a form of separation that, in contrast to French laicism, entails supportive rather than skeptical treatment of all religions by the state. In contrast to Europe, with its state-supported territorial religious monopolies, the politically or theologically dissatisfied in the United States never had to withdraw into a marginal culture or counterculture; they could always find a place in the rich spectrum of religious communities. As a result these religious communities are geared more towards a market and less towards the state. Key actors tend to be entrepreneurial rather than bureaucratic. Churches have no qualms about handing out questionnaires to measure their members' or potential members' levels of satisfaction. Since members' willingness to donate money is of crucial significance to church communities' existence, it is tapped with great professionalism. Market-like conditions foster attempts to found new "enterprises." Rather than waiting passively for individuals to show an interest in joining, religious communities actively seek to forge connections between the religious life of the church and people's interests (such as those of migrants). This entails dangers and abuses that can be every bit as bad as those of official bureaucratic churches. The least disturbing of these is so-called church shopping, which refers to individuals' openness (when moving house, for example) to joining a new religious community because of its appealing social or spiritual offerings. But this occurs almost exclusively in the Protestant spectrum and is facilitated by the perception that the theological differences between the many Protestant denominations are increasingly irrelevant. Conversely, I consider it disturbing when religious communities talk up faith as such or membership in their church in particular as a means of achieving preconceived goals. They may claim to provide a magic bullet for fulfilling hopes of wealth, a slim figure, physical beauty, or political power. The important point here though is that the legal and economic conditions for the action of religious communities must be taken into account in examining the secularizing effects of modernization. Just as important, however, is whether the demonstrable plurality of religious communities is itself perceived as valuable, in other words, whether there is a commitment to the value of pluralism. What is crucial in the case of the United States, then, is not just the existence of a market in religious options but the firm institutionalization of religious freedom in connection with a different understanding of the role of the state.

3. Simply considering the United States can unsettle a Eurocentric perspective. The notion of rule and exception loses its plausibility. If we adopt a consistently global historical perspective, the notion of the nineteenth century as an era of comprehensive secularization becomes completely untenable. Instead, we find that this period was one of the triumphant expansion of religion.[17] There are two key factors that a Eurocentric perspective overlooks: the religious consequences of European expansion in the nineteenth century and the impact of the technological innovations of this period on non-European religions.

Of course, European expansion did not begin during this period, but it did achieve significantly greater intensity during it; it was often bound up with missionary projects. It is difficult to briefly sum up the effects of missionization and colonialism, but it is immediately apparent that nothing could be a less appropriate description than "secularization." In Africa and parts of Latin America Christianity (and in Africa Islam as well) spread further, though "from above," and it was only after the inculcation of faith over generations that it truly became rooted in a given culture. In Asia, colonialism and missionary work tended to encounter cultures and religions that considered themselves superior to the intruders but also felt threatened by them. Here we find a spectrum of responses ranging from the reinterpretation of indigenous religious traditions in such a way as to make them more like Christianity, to radical opposition. Particularly in the cases of Hinduism and Confucianism, studies have described how they were constructed as religions in the Western sense only in the face of the Christian-colonialist challenge.[18] The use of printing technology by missionaries and the building of churches revolutionized the use of media and building techniques among the non-Christian religions. To understand the development of religion in the twentieth century, the development of the state in the postcolonial age and the specific relationship between state and religion in postcolonial societies are also of great importance. In the case of Latin America we find a transition from a generally state-supported Catholic monopoly to religious pluralism; in Africa, the failed or absent consolidation of the postcolonial state is proving crucial to the role of religious communities.[19]

4. Exponents of the thesis of secularization tend to greatly overstate actual religiosity in Europe prior to the processes described as secularization. It is certainly true that there have been repeated historical phases of extreme religious intensity. As many sources demonstrate, however, knowledge of the Christian faith even among the clergy, but especially among the laity, was often lamentably if not grotesquely underdeveloped. Many of the efforts to supervise and educate made in the context of the so-called Counter-Reformation can only be understood in light of these shortcomings. Often, only a small part of the population attended church services, and churches were frequently hard to reach. Laws requiring participation in church services would have been superfluous if people had come of their own volition. Hatred of the clergy's real or imagined privileges, views that diverged greatly from official doctrine, magical reinterpretations of the sacraments, and religious apathy were very common, not least in the countryside. The image of a popular piety upheld by an

upright and ingenuous populace is a romantic idealization of the past. Many commentators have expressed doubts that it was possible for Europe to be as strongly de-Christianized as asserted in the thesis of secularization—since in many respects it had only been superficially and imperfectly Christianized in the first place and pre-Christian forms frequently endured: "Christ stopped at Eboli."[20] This evaluation can still be found today though the simplistic division between popular and elite religiosity has been replaced by complex models of exchange between the two.[21] In England, although industrialization initially plunged religious communities into crisis, it eventually led to a general increase in religious practices and growing church membership compared with the preindustrial period. This was not the case everywhere,[22] but even in Germany, where a significant number of urban workers turned away from the churches, those who remained committed during this period generally had church doctrine instilled in them all the more thoroughly.

From all four perspectives, when we subject the secularization thesis to historical-sociological examination, it emerges as highly questionable. Modernization is by no means necessarily linked with secularization and, as we shall see, secularization often occurs without modernization. This also alters our perception of those European cases that lend superficial plausibility to the secularization thesis. This thesis fails to explain even these cases. There, too, the true causes for secularization must be factors other than modernization. Among these causes is the secularization thesis itself. In the strongly secularized countries, it is common to regard religion as something that is *still* present and to shake one's head in wonder that it is *still* there. Many people today chuckle when they refer to their religious childhood and youth, their time as altar servers for example, as if to a curiosity, a closed chapter in biographical and historical terms that provides no vibrant option for the present or future. After the overview provided here, however, it is surely difficult to go on believing in any law-like connection between modernization and secularization. As usual in the history of science, if a paradigm that has long ruled the roost is struck by crisis, it does not vanish overnight. Some reject it entirely; others attempt to save it through modifications, perhaps merely by making excuses for it. But the secularization thesis has lost the power to become a self-fulfilling prophecy. This is the nucleus of an epochal shift.

2

Does Secularization Lead
to Moral Decline?

There have been wide-ranging public debates on religion and ethics, on the significance of faith to the mediation of values and social cohesion, and on the risks arising from religions for tolerance and peaceful coexistence. All these debates tend to be marred by empirical deficiencies. Contributors typically argue in what we might describe as an "a priori" fashion. What I mean is that in light of a supposed essence of religion in general, or the Christian faith in particular, they infer that these phenomena are indispensable or dangerous; the same goes for those who draw similarly far-reaching conclusions in light of their understanding of reason as such and thus seek to demonstrate the superiority of a rational moral justification, or declare that the goal of their arguments is to demonstrate the fundamental limits of such justifications.

I have no wish to cast any fundamental aspersions on the complex philosophical arguments that have been put forward on both sides, but I do propose that we proceed in a more empirically focused way. An "empirical" approach, of course, does not mean naïvely assuming that we can come up with uncontested solutions to philosophical issues, with their inevitably normative dimensions, on the basis of factual accounts. What I mean by "empirical" here is an attitude entailing a minimum of conceptual prejudices, one that goes beyond the a priori and is open to the richness of historical-cultural phenomena. As far as this attitude is concerned, my role model in the field of religion and values is the great American pragmatist philosopher and psychologist William James, and especially his classic *The Varieties of Religious Experience* (1902).[1] In this book, he first sought to distance himself from every dogmatic presupposition in the field of religious studies—whether theological or secularist in character—simply by refraining from taking religious doctrines or institutions as his point of departure, and focusing instead on the dynamics of religious experience, which are merely interpreted in religious teachings, and placed on a permanent basis and organized through religious institutions. So he had already selected a point of departure beyond the opposition between "believers" and "nonbelievers," since from this perspective even nonbelievers have at least imaginative access to the experiences he analyzed, which in my own writings I call experiences of self-transcendence.[2] In carrying out his study, James was also very careful to give each of his statements a fundamentally fallible, in other words empirically refutable or supersedable, status. When he underlined that the greatest examples of asceticism and heroic acts of moral decentering had so far been found exclusively among religiously motivated individuals, for instance, he expressed this in such a way as to avoid dogmatically ruling out the possibility that nonreligious individuals might perform similar feats of asceticism and moral heroism in future, or that there might already have been such cases in the past that had received insufficient attention. The twentieth century, with its "heroic" deeds in service to secular ideals, such as the nation, the victory of the supposed Aryan race, or Communism, would no doubt have prompted James to modify his thesis; my own response would be to refer to sacredness where James referred to religious motivation, making it clear that the sacredness of ideals and the resulting emotional energies may also be associated with secular content.[3]

But when it comes to contemporary religious controversies, this "empirical-philosophical" attitude (Arnold Gehlen) makes sense, not just for general methodological reasons, but also for a special reason connected with the present-day religious-political constellation. One of this book's key ideas is that the historical moment in which we find ourselves and in which we argue about religious issues is characterized by the death of two seeming certainties. The first of these apparent certainties was the subject of the first chapter. Most secularists since the eighteenth century had assumed that history was on their side and that modernization, in the sense of economic growth and scientific-technological progress, inevitably leads to the weakening of religion and in the long run even to its disappearance. This notion, which intellectuals derived primarily from the history of France and perhaps a few other countries in Western Europe, and which sometimes took the form of a violent state ideology in Marxist-ruled nations in the twentieth century, has virtually collapsed over the past two decades for both internal and external reasons. I shall not be delving further into the internal reasons associated with such a cognitivist or functionalist understanding of religious faith. Of the external reasons for this collapse, the most important is the growing understanding that the claimed connection between modernization and secularization is not being repeated outside of Europe, with the exception of a small number of so-called settler societies (New Zealand, Uruguay, and so on). In light of this, the United States, with its tremendous religious vitality, is viewed less and less as a special case in need of explanation. Whatever the specific details, modernization in other parts of the globe is not leading to secularization either, and the history of European secularization thus looks increasingly like a contingent process. Of course, these empirical findings need not prevent anyone from welcoming and supporting processes of secularization. But now that the thesis of secularization is a thing of the past, secularism must make do without guarantees anchored in a philosophy of history and must be justified by something other than a narrative of progress.

But I referred to the end of two seeming certainties. It is important to avoid any triumphalist undertone when claiming that the thesis of secularization is a thing of the past. Instead, we must immediately add that the old religious apologist counterthesis also seems to have met its end. While secularists are only too happy to believe the secularization thesis, believers have tended to claim that faith is indispensable to mental health, moral motivation, and/or social cohesion, at least since religious faith as such was forced onto the defensive through the rise of the secular option. To a degree, then, they warn that secularization represents a danger to health, morality, and peace.

But it seems to me that this thesis too has run out of steam for both internal and external reasons. By internal reasons I mean the following insight, which I consider irrefutable. There may be empirically demonstrable connections between religion and mental health, moral orientation, and so on, which stands to reason simply because religions advise people against certain risky and antisocial behaviors and offer them alternatives. But no one is going to embrace faith on the basis of rational insights into these connections. The mere idea that this is possible would degrade religious faith to the status of autosuggestion therapy. By "external" reasons I mean that the present-day emergence of largely secularized societies in a sense allows us to test empirically religious apologists' predictions. When nineteenth-century commentators stated that without faith in God, everything would be allowed, and morality and social cohesion would therefore become impossible, no secularized societies yet existed; there were just a few scattered national liberal and proletarian milieus featuring a hostility to or distance from religion. It is only since the late 1960s in parts of Western Europe and since the late 1950s in most parts of Eastern Europe outside of the Soviet Union that we can refer to strongly secularized societies. In this sense, broadly based secularization is the historical novelty.

However—to put it in the style of William James—so far, moral decline has not occurred in the most affected societies (formerly Communist ones such as eastern Germany, the Czech Republic, and Estonia, and Western ones such as the United Kingdom, Sweden, and so on). Just as the lack of secularization in the modernizing world outside of Europe speaks against the thesis of secularization, the lack of moral decline in strongly secularized European societies contradicts the idea that secularization will tend to wreck morality. In public debates, people are always very quick to diagnose loss of faith as the cause of crimes and abuses—such as shocking cases of child murder, juvenile delinquency, or corruption—but as social science this is clearly amateurish stuff. In order to lay claim to causal validity, statements of this kind would require corroboration from historical or international comparisons, and I know of no serious study that has done this. On the contrary, we often find corruption in highly religious societies as well—we need only think of the "amoral familism" of southern Italy (Edward Banfield). According to many indicators, notwithstanding the intensity of religious life in United States described earlier, the level of violence in the United States is about five times the European average.[4] Notwithstanding that "a significant amount of research has shown that moderately religious Americans report greater subjective well-being and life satisfaction, greater marital satisfaction, better family cohesion, and fewer symptoms of depression than the nonreligious,"[5] some comparative studies have concluded "that nations with high rates of belief in God also had high rates of homicide, juvenile and early adult mortality, STD infections, teen pregnancy, and abortion than nations in which belief in God is relatively low."[6] Mere correlations between religion and criminality and so on are ill-suited to answering causal questions. At first sight, it does not seem possible to provide causal explanations of moral shortcomings with reference to religion, in either a positive or negative sense.

So my question as to whether there is unambiguous empirical evidence that secularization leads to moral decline can "so far" be answered straightforwardly in the negative. But more interesting than this finding is reflection on the reasons for it. Refutation of the secularization thesis may prompt us to reflect on what faith actually consists of and to consider how we might revise our notion of modernization if we no longer consider secularization to be its inevitable corollary. In much the same way, the increasing implausibility of the idea that secularization is a morally destructive force may prompt us to contemplate the connection between morality and religion in a new way.

I would like to do this now in four steps. I first ask whether morality in secularized societies might merely be the lingering echo of religious traditions. With reference to tribal societies, I then briefly examine whether the notion of the constitutive role of religion for morality is valid in the first place. Looking at an example from Christian missionary work, I go on to briefly examine the interaction between new religions and traditional morality. To conclude, I fuse these reflections into a hypothesis about the two origins of normative regulation and identify the one area in which I myself currently see a risk of moral regression through secularization.

Morality as lingering echo?

Since secularization, particularly that of women, is a fairly recent historical phenomenon,[7] it is practically impossible to make an empirically grounded statement about its long-term effects, over several generations, on moral orientations, if we want to go beyond the most superficial level—namely, normative attitudes to specific lifestyle issues in which there is a pronounced difference between church doctrine and the contemporary consensus (as in the case of contraception). It is fairly easy to measure such attitudes. If, on the other hand, we are interested in deeper structures of moral judgment, we have to take a detour and scrutinize these, along with the persistence of religiously molded differences such as confessional specificities, over a given period of time. One of the most interesting studies of this kind comes from Andrew Greeley.[8] Building on the work of the leading Chicago theologian David Tracy, he distinguishes dichotomously between the Protestant and Catholic "imaginations," in other words, confessionally molded worldviews. The claim here is that these worldviews produce theological and ethical codes, but are themselves prepropositional and metaphorical. On this assumption, differences in particular teachings and ethical conceptions are not the truly definitive level of distinction between the confessions, but merely manifestations of a more fundamental difference in their dominant symbolism. Tracy calls these distinctions "analogical" versus "dialectical." The analogical "Catholic" worldview assumes a God who shows Himself in and through His creation, such that everything in the world participates in the divine; the Protestant worldview, conversely, sees the world as radically distinct from God, such that God reveals Himself only rarely in the world, particularly through Jesus Christ. For Catholics, so the argument goes, natural social relations are themselves testimony to the presence of God in the world; for Protestants, meanwhile, the individual is only fully human in her or his voluntary relationship with God, while society is distant from God. The idea here is that these contrasting notions of individuality and sociality in turn form the point of departure for very different attitudes to the role of institutionalized religion and to a whole range of ethical and political issues. These differences are particularly vivid in the field of child-rearing: "Protestants will value in their children the virtues of initiative, integrity, industry, and thrift more than Catholics, while Catholics will value loyalty, obedience, and patience. Protestants will be especially likely to deplore vices which diminish personal integrity, honesty, and sense of duty. Catholics will be especially likely to be offended by actions which seem to violate relationship networks—adultery, prostitution, suicide."[9] We might also underline that the role of intentions seems to vary between the confessions—namely, with respect to whether good intentions or actions themselves are decisive in evaluating the moral quality of an action; and that the status of moral statements is understood differently depending on whether these are viewed as norms or as ideals.

It is quite clear, and both Tracy and Greeley are fully aware of this, that the major theological disputes within Christianity cannot really be schematized in such a simplistic, dichotomous way. We should also note that in describing Protestantism, these authors clearly had in mind the varieties dominant in the English-speaking world, and that German or Scandinavian Lutheranism occupies an intermediate position here. But none of this is of primary concern to us. What matters here is the persistence of such deep-rooted religious "imaginations." What emerged from the "International Study of Values" in the 1980s is that in twenty-one of the thirty-six variables examined, there are statistically significant connections between denomination and value-orientation, all of them of the kind we might expect. There were no contradictory correlations. In every country examined, Protestants emphasized freedom and individualism, while Catholics tended to highlight equality, fairness, and so forth. The differences were more pronounced in the English-speaking countries than in continental Europe, although to highly varying degrees. They emerged as less pronounced in the United States compared with the United Kingdom, Ireland, Canada, and Australia, which may be linked with ethnic differences and the way these are imbued with confessional significance (and vice versa) in all these countries (with the exception of Australia). But most important for our purposes is the finding that these differences do not decrease if we consider only younger respondents.[10] We can therefore rule out the possibility that new generations of individuals of faith will exhibit a fundamental value shift, such that their new attitudes are no longer nourished by the fundamental imaginaries deeply entrenched in their religious worldview.

But if this is true, and in such a way that those affected are quite unaware of it, then it is probable that such entrenched imaginaries have an influence even on those individuals who have broken away from the religious orientations that have shaped them. In this case we would not simply be dealing with a secular worldview that can be contrasted with religious worldviews. This would mean that the origins of secular worldviews in a religious imagination would still be very much a part of these world-views—whether because apparently taken-for-granted elements of the religious worldview are passed on through secularization or whether because a specific rejection of elements of the religious worldview is decisive to a particular secular worldview through a process of disidentification. There is a wide range of secularisms, just as there is a wide range of religions.

This assumption would make sense of observations that present the strongly secularized moral and political culture of Sweden, for example, as thoroughly Lutheran Protestant, or Soviet Stalinism, in terms, for example, of its imagery, as rooted in many respects in the models of Orthodox Christianity. (There is also the famous story of a man crossing the dividing line between Catholics and Protestants in a Northern Irish city who is asked at gunpoint which religion he is. He answers that he is an atheist. He is then asked: a Catholic or Protestant atheist?) So there appears to be a persistence of fundamental structures of morally relevant perception across long periods of time, such that even under conditions of secularization an older imagination may continue to guide morality—if secularization does not deploy coercion and violence against specific phenomena derived from this imagination.

In line with this, we cannot yet make an empirically secure statement about what the moral impact of mass secularization across many generations might be. If we wish to do so, we would have to consider two other perspectives. First, the motive for secularism may be highly moral. It is ridiculous when so-called new atheists such as Richard Dawkins and Daniel Dennett treat religious people as stupid and limited, but it is, of course, equally ridiculous when evangelical propagandists in the United States seek to show that atheists are "arbitrary, unreasonable, ignorant, inconsistent, irresponsible, disreputable, uncaring, or, especially, immoral."[11] After all, the great atheists of the nineteenth century often fought Christianity because they saw the hope of life in the hereafter as detracting attention from improving life in this world and as an obstacle to living life intensely or because they suspected Christian morality of entailing unnecessary guilt feelings, the compulsive rejection of one's own physicality, and hypocrisy in interpersonal behavior. These views, however justified or unjustified they may be, obviously express deeply moral motives. The same applies to those today who argue against religion, as long as their arguments are informed by more than blind ideology and they show a genuine interest in faith as it is lived. Typical in present-day Germany, however, is a naïve, routinized, habitual atheism. As early as 1895, Max Weber's friend and rival Ernst Troeltsch asserted that atheistic ethics would have the consequences it promises only if judged by a specific religious ethics that it aims to overcome. In the absence of this comparative perspective, Troeltsch argued, it frequently loses its power to motivate and its noble characteristics.[12] Developments in the still strongly secular countries of post-Communist Europe in particular seem to me to confirm Troeltsch's claim. But without distinguishing the moral depth of various forms of atheism, we cannot make statements about the moral consequences of secularization.

In addition, recent American studies show that in the United States the vast majority of children who did not grow up in a religious environment develop religious commitments over the course of their lives.[13] To speak in sociological terms, the religiously unattached have one of the lowest "retention rates"; even the minority of those who were raised without affiliation to religion and who have not yet joined religious communities as adults leave open the possibility that this might change. In the vast majority of cases, they do not see themselves as staunch atheists, but as not having found the right religious community yet. This applies only to the markedly religious United States and not to the secularized societies of Europe, although the significant role of Christian schools in post-Communist eastern Germany may be regarded as opening up new possibilities in a near-homogeneously secular setting. In any case, this demonstrates that the question of the moral consequences of secularization changes if we are prepared to go beyond the idea of secularization as an irreversible process. In a highly religious society, the lack of faith may be a merely generational phenomenon without long-term effects. But even in societies that came under extreme pressure to secularize for a certain time (such as the People's Republic of China), dramatic processes of religious revitalization cannot be ruled out.

A nonreligious source of morality

We began by discussing the fact that moral orientations are often nourished by a deep layer of imagination that resists easy conceptualization. The following examination of morality in "tribal societies," on the other hand, makes a different point. The aim here is to demonstrate that there are basic structures of lived reciprocity that themselves represent a source of morality and as such are not determined by the religious imagination.

I would like to demonstrate this with reference to Bronislaw Malinowski's classic study from the 1920s, *Crime and Custom in Savage Society.*[14] Years of research among the Trobriand Islanders of Melanesia prompted Malinowski to take issue with two notions that had previously dominated, namely, that "savages," as the term itself suggests, know no laws or, if laws exist, they follow them "but fitfully and loosely,"[15] and the idea that in "tribes," the sense of the group is so strong that there must be total obedience to custom and tradition, which extend into the minutiae of everyday life. Malinowski countered both ideas, often espoused by researchers with no first-hand knowledge of tribal life, with a study that begins with the economic sphere—specifically collective fishing. He describes in detail how collective fishing at sea requires the use of large canoes in which a large number of men must work together. All expect a share when the catch is divided up. "Thus the ownership and use of the canoe consist of a series of definitive obligations and duties uniting a group of people into a working team."[16] It emerges that there is in fact a "definite system of division of functions and a rigid system of mutual obligations, into which a sense of duty and the recognition of the need of co-operation enter side by side with a realization of self-interest, privileges and benefits. . . . It is the sum of duties, privileges and mutualities which bind the joint owners to the object and to each other."[17] A mechanism similar to that between the cooperating fishermen can also be observed in the relationship between the fishing villages and their inland counterparts. Complex relations of exchange are maintained—namely, vegetables for fish, distributed in line with an annual cycle—in which each community "has, therefore, a weapon for the enforcement of its rights: reciprocity."[18] The exchange partners are in fact often linked together on several levels—including marriage relations. Like all rules of reciprocity resting on considerations of utility, these too constantly run the risk of noncompliance—of free riding. But the regulations are elastic and allow considerable room for interpretation and compliance. Malinowski comes to the conclusion that alongside a religiously grounded penal law, which was the sole concern of the great French sociologist Emile Durkheim in his classic work on the history of the division of labor,[19] reciprocity is the foundation of the entire social structure. As important as the quasi-penal law of these "primitives" may be, it is not everything; they also have a quasi-civil law: "There must be in all societies a class of rules too practical to be backed up by religious sanctions, too burdensome to be left to mere goodwill, too personally vital to individuals to be enforced by any abstract agency."[20]

As it happens, the step taken here by Malinowski converged with the insights into the fundamental importance of *giving* to the establishment and maintenance of social relations in the work of his friend and Durkheim's nephew Marcel Mauss. Giving is not solely geared towards utility, as in the case of exchange, nor purely charitable, but it is constitutive of relationships.[21] These studies represent a kind of phylogenetic counterpart to the ontogenetic findings in the developmental psychology of Jean Piaget, Lawrence Kohlberg, and their students. Their work too shows that children may "discover" fundamental moral rules—such as fairness in games—independently and without the involvement of educational authorities, namely, by reflecting on the conditions for successful shared play.[22] Without going into these famous studies in detail, we can safely say that social reciprocity is itself a source of morality, one that is not grounded in religious imaginaries, and will therefore probably not be directly affected by processes of secularization.

Moral decline through religion?

But there are limits to reciprocity. First, direct reciprocity can suffice only under very simple conditions, which, of course, did not even pertain in the tribal society described by Malinowski. If a third party joins the chain of interaction *a-b-c,* there is already a problem of circulation and guarantees. If I expect an adequate quid pro quo, not from my immediate counterpart, but from a third party and only after a temporal delay, this opens up new potential for deviation, and trust in the maintenance of norms becomes more important. Many schools of thought informed by models of utility-oriented action are now examining these issues in depth.[23]

Second, there are limits to reciprocity set by the finitude of our lives. My favorite attempt to convey this comes from the American baseball legend Yogi Berra: "Always go to other people's funerals, otherwise they won't come to yours." Why should we feel obliged to pass on to our children the love we received from our parents? This is the point at which many assert that a morality of reciprocity is necessarily unstable and requires an additional, *religious* foundation.

I find this idea plausible in the sense that additional value commitments that are long-term and not situation-dependent, such as the value of justice, can certainly help prevent utility-oriented refusals of reciprocity such as free riding. But in the first instance such a value commitment need be no more than an attachment to the reflexively understood rules of fair cooperation as such—for example, through commitment to the golden rule or, one level of reflection higher, the categorical imperative. Even if it is wrong, as Kant is often assumed to have believed, and as the early Habermas did in fact believe, that the force of rational motivation in this sense is strong and sufficient, this does not mean that only a religious motivation can provide stability. A powerful force of this kind may be generally inherent in strong, experientially saturated values, including those that have emerged from experiences of a negative kind. The subjective self-evidence of the intolerable nature of suffering and degradation may certainly lead to a desire for revenge and spirals of violence but also, conversely, to an attachment to values such as human dignity and non-violence—and from a historical-empirical point of view, this obviously applies to individuals with no religious commitment as well. The history of human rights exhibits a complex interplay between the religious and secular. This history cannot be adequately understood as Christian or anti-Christian.[24]

In addition, it is by no means inevitable that religions will provide moral reinforcement for society's fundamental structures of reciprocity. To illustrate this, I turn to a literary example, although one of an almost ethnological character. I am thinking of the story *On the Edge of the World* (1875–76) by the great Russian Christian writer Nikolai Leskov,[25] which explores the failures of Russian Orthodox missionary work in Siberia and Central Asia. The frame narrative initially suggests that the Orthodox missionaries' lack of success in comparison to the Protestant ones recently allowed into the Russian Empire from abroad can only be the result of the Russian clergy's low level of education and slow-wittedness. But then a bishop relates how he has tried to uncover these shortcomings through tours of inspection. To his surprise, he discovers that it is the best and brightest clergy who, after some time, tend to suffer the greatest doubts about missionary work. Caught in a terrible blizzard, the bishop has the first-hand and poignant experience of receiving help from an unbaptized tribesman, while a priest traveling with him is cruelly abandoned to his fate by another tribesman who has been baptized. He learns that individual baptism detaches members of the tribe from their social obligations, prompting one of them to undergo baptism repeatedly under different names on others' behalf in order to spare them the same fate of losing others' trust. Above all, he learns that the newly baptized may cite confession to justify their abandonment of obligations of reciprocity. While they would formerly have made compensation for misdeeds as a matter of course, they now believe that confession has relieved them of this need. It is, of course, easy to dismiss this as a simple misunderstanding of confession and baptism—but what Leskov wants to show is that much of what is considered a missionary success cannot be justified if we truly understand the Christian message. Here it is not secularization but missionary work that leads to moral decline. And this problem is not limited to tribal societies. If faith in Christ is torn from all contexts of tradition and community, it is inevitably diluted to the point where it becomes a mere individualistic recipe for salvation, which suggests morally destructive consequences in itself.[26]

Two origins of morality

We may sum up these empirically based reflections on the alleged indispensability of religion to morality as follows. So far, secularization cannot be shown to lead to moral decline. This may be due in part to the persistence of moral orientations that emanate from a religious imagination, but that retain their strength despite being detached from their seedbed. But what seems crucial here is that the structures of human cooperation themselves either lead individuals to uphold reciprocal obligations for reasons of self-interest or open their minds to the value of justice. This and other morally relevant values may inspire commitment through positive experiences, of their embodiment in role models, for example, or in negative experiences, such as the experience of injustice, denigration, or violence. As I argued in the final chapter of my book *The Genesis of Values*, in human history morality has always had two roots: values and value-constitutive experiences, on the one hand, and reflection on the conditions of cooperation, on the other.[27] Specific systems of norms are derived from both sources, through the concretization of values and through abstraction from cooperation. It is certainly true that in their specific action situations, actors must take account of both the good and the right. Reduction to the right is just as one-sided as reduction to the good; also impermissible is reduction of the good to the religiously imperative.

Because of this, while in principle I shared many of the aims of the failed 2006–9 "Pro Reli" ballot initiative in Berlin (for the compulsory teaching of religion in Berlin schools), I could not agree with the slogan "Values Need God." Certainly, believers cannot articulate their values without reference to their faith; but this articulation of faith should be an invitation to nonbelievers at least to consider their values, if not their faith; it should not deny them the possibility of finding their way to these values through routes other than this faith. It seems to me that the most important front running through moral and political disputes today is not that between believers and nonbelievers but that between universalists and anti-universalists, and both of these groups include both religious and nonreligious people. Personally, while it is true that the universalist potential of Christianity is always permanently at risk, I see in the Gospel the strongest "imagination" of universalism ever bestowed upon humanity. I know that others ascribe to Kant's philosophy or other forms of philosophical argument a similar status and thus conceive of them not so much as the articulation of historically generated values, as I do, but as their rational justification, conceived at a particular point in time yet valid across time and situation-independent. For such people, thinkers such as Kant or Habermas are charismatic figures. For them, rather than solving an intellectual problem, these thinkers laid down a moral foundation. Endowing Kant's work with such meaning seems to me to do justice neither to him nor to the possible range of argumentational justifications in general. We can, of course, argue about the different meaning of justification with respect to religious faith or rational argument. My concern is not that secularization destroys morality as such, but that weakening Christianity weakens one of the pillars of moral and legal universalism. If this universalism came into the world historically in association with notions of transcendence, as asserted in Karl Jaspers's Axial Age thesis,[28] it is not certain that it will ultimately survive the loss of these notions, of their original basis. But a concern is not the same as a battle cry.

3

Waves of Secularization

When the French king Louis XV fell seriously ill in 1744, he vowed that if he were to recover, he would build a new church in Paris and consecrate it to Sainte Geneviève. He did in fact get better, but the French state's strained finances and technical difficulties in laying the foundations caused such severe delays that the church had not been completed when the king died in 1774; it had yet to be consecrated when the French Revolution broke out in 1789. This situation prompted the decision by the revolutionary National Assembly in 1791 to use the planned neoclassical church for a different purpose under a different name. It was now to commemorate the great men of the nation and would be known as the Panthéon. The mortal remains of Mirabeau, Voltaire, and Rousseau were transferred there, and all religious symbols were removed. After Napoleon had brought the Revolution to an end, however, it was decided that there would be a church of Sainte Geneviève after all, and the inscription from the days of the revolution gave way to a cross. Once again, however, the political regime came to an end before the measures needed to open the church could be taken; it was finally opened only in 1822. Just eight years later, in the July Revolution of 1830, another reversal occurred. But not for the last time. In 1851–52, Napoleon III decreed that the building would be used as a church again. The wooden cross was again placed atop the dome. But it was fated to be sawed off by communards in 1871. After the uprising had been put down, a new cross was erected, this time of stone, in 1873. Finally, in 1885, following the death of Victor Hugo, the spectacular building was again turned into a Panthéon of great men, but this time there was no attempt to remove the cross. In the words of the British historian Owen Chadwick, to whom I owe this story, this building "became a sign of de-Christianizing revolution, national virtues instead of old virtues, La France instead of Sainte Geneviève; and because it became a sign, it was buffeted to and fro in accordance with the see-saw of party politics, holy and secular, holy and secular, until at last, like so much of Western Europe, it lay almost secularized, but with the not so old stone cross still there to make a memory and a blessing, the past of Europe still speaking to the present, and keeping guard over men once thought to be the vilest enemies of the cross, but now seen to have fought for freedom and for truths that were necessary to the human spirit."[1]

We can draw two very different conclusions from this brief history of a building so familiar to visitors to Paris. One narrative we might believe confirmed here is that secularization is a movement that began in the eighteenth century with thinkers such as Voltaire, expanded to include an increasing number of enlightened figures and population groups, and became ever more powerful over the course of time. Despite all the temporary setbacks and the resistance of reactionary forces, its historical triumph ultimately proved inevitable. But a very different narrative is also possible and compatible with the facts of the Panthéon's history. This alternative narrative would emphasize that secularization in Europe was never a linear, continuous, uniform process. Instead, we are dealing with a highly conflictual, heterogeneous, contingent history. In this chapter I aim to defend this second interpretation against its more widespread alternative by taking the temporal dimension of secularization more seriously than is usually done in secularization theory. My main hypothesis is that secularization, where it occurred, did so in "waves," and that we can get closer to understanding its causes if we take a closer look at these waves—of secularization, but also of religious revitalization.

As set out in chapter 1, over the past few years and in a wide variety of ways, many sociologists of religion, including myself,[2] have sought to demonstrate the untenable nature of the conventional thesis of secularization, according to which processes of modernization more or less automatically lead to secularization. There is no need to repeat these arguments here or to comment upon the complexities of these debates or the ambiguity of the key terms ("modernization"/"secularization"), which is done in other chapters. At least since the era in which most social science disciplines emerged, that is, since the late nineteenth century, the thesis of secularization has been so dominant that those espousing it have often seemed freed from the obligation to refer to any kind of evidence, and this hegemony intensified in the decades after World War II. At present, however, among the eminent scholars on the subject only a minority (Pippa Norris and Ronald Inglehart; Steve Bruce; Detlef Pollack) continue to defend this thesis with reference to old and new empirical evidence. The majority of scholars are now looking for alternative models to portray religious change and alternative vocabularies to describe the contemporary religious situation.

As we go about this search, I believe it is crucial that the weakening of the secularization thesis does not cause us to lose sight of the phenomenon of secularization. It would be a mistake merely to keep extending the definition of religion in such a way as to exclude the possibility of secularization on a conceptual level, that is, simply to subsume an increasing number of phenomena under the term "religion." Whatever our precise definition of secularization, and however we measure and evaluate religious practices, attitudes, or membership, there can be no doubt that a significant portion of contemporary Europe and a small number of non-European societies are profoundly secular. It is important to point out here that all secularized societies, to modify Tolstoy's famous phrase at the beginning of *Anna Karenina*, are secularized "in their own way." The writings of Grace Davie have, for example, popularized the plausible term "vicarious religion" to describe the situation in the highly secularized societies of Scandinavia.[3] This refers to a situation in which religion is often "performed by an active minority but on behalf of a much larger number, who (implicitly, at least) not only understand, but approve of what the minority is doing."[4] In the case of highly secularized formerly Communist societies such as that of eastern Germany, however, this concept fails to get to the heart of the matter. It would fly in the face of reality to pretend that the atheistic majority there somehow feels it is being represented by the various religious minorities. So overcoming the thesis of secularization does not mean ignoring secularization. It means grasping its diverse forms.

An alternative explanation of religious decline

We cannot explain the unfolding of secularization processes and the range of forms this process can take if we conceive of secularization simply as resulting from progress in knowledge and economic growth. We must instead focus on the institutional arrangements straddling state, economy, and religious communities. The crucial dimension in explaining processes of secularization—this at least is my argument—is the attitude of churches and other religious communities or organizations to a number of key issues: the so-called national, social, and democratic questions, the rights of the individual and religious pluralism. The effects of economic, scientific, or cultural developments on religion, like the impulses emanating from religious doubt or experiences of religious certainty, are always mediated by these fields of tension. It is this that gives them their secularizing or desecularizing force.

David Martin developed a typology of religious-political constellations in the 1970s on the basis of much historical research, pioneering this analytical method. His typology paved the way for the historically sensitive analysis of secularization in light of its internal diversity and causes. Unfortunately, however, Martin's book *A General Theory of Secularization* is, to quote Kevin Christiano, "one of the most gloriously mistitled works in our field."[5] It is certainly not what its title claims, at least not if we assume that a general theory must make clear statements about the connections between causal variables and their effects. In fact Martin's "theory" was an attempt to glean generalizing statements from the study and comparison of historical cases that nonetheless retain all the richness of their historical specificity. In this sense, we might describe his approach as "Weberian" and identify Max Weber as its true progenitor. But this is no good, since Max Weber made many statements about long-term tendencies in the development of religion (progressive "disenchantment" and "rationalization") that are not covered by the method described above and are instead rooted in his complex personal relationship to Protestant Christianity.[6] These statements by Weber have, moreover, become the stuff of public discussion, far more than his empirical analyses. In our time, one of the most important contributions that broadly accords with my own views is that of the American sociologist Christian Smith, who applies social scientific knowledge about the genesis of social movements and how revolutions unfold to the analysis of secularization processes.[7] Smith is interested primarily in the diminishing public role of religion, rather than secularization in the sense of a weakening of religion, and he defines religion in terms of the supernatural, not in terms of the sacred as I do, but his work is highly instructive in the present context. He refuses to look at secularization in isolation from social struggles. But if we make this connection, then the individual and collective actors involved, their motives and interests, ideas and objectives, resources and opportunity structures, strategies and organizations move to center stage. It goes without saying that we must also consider the unintended consequences of social processes, but however much we may emphasize the unique character of religion, this inevitably means that we are paving the way for a political sociology of its development. From this perspective, secularization theory is the ideology of the victors in struggles over secularization.

I would like to add a remark on the most ambitious explanatory project of recent times: Charles Taylor's' monumental *A Secular Age*. It is certainly a masterpiece of historical writing, but Taylor is primarily interested in the philosophical and cultural preconditions for the rise of what he fittingly calls the "secular option." In my view, however, there are two different explanatory issues here that must be clearly separated from one another. First, we must explain how the secular option became available, and, second, we must explain why this option, as soon as it became available, proved so attractive to some and so repugnant to others—why, in other words, this option was embraced to such different degrees by different national or regional milieus, social strata, genders, and generations. It seems to me that Taylor avoids this second task, along with other explanatory issues (in the social scientific sense) when he introduces concepts such as the "nova effect" for the ongoing multiplication of religious and secular options—as if options could increase of their own accord. We find much the same problem when he ascribes a linear trajectory to the periodic impulse for reform in medieval Christianity and refers to a long-term vector of Latin Christianity, for which, however, he is unable to offer any explanation.[8]

As I have said, my thesis, based on the method of analysis set out above, is that secularization occurs in waves. In the European history of secularization—and the history of secularization is in large part a European history—I believe we can identify three such waves. Two of them, the first and the third, consist of just a few years. The starting point for the first was in France and gained traction there, although not only there, in the years after 1791. It lasted until around 1803. The third wave occurred in Western Europe between 1969 and 1973. Both waves (of the 1790s and 1970s) are transnational European phenomena. The second wave is less compressed temporally and as such is not a transnational phenomenon, but rather a pattern bound up with the consequences of industrialization and urbanization in the nineteenth century. But these consequences played themselves out in different regions and societies during different periods of time. I shall limit myself here to remarks on these three waves, leaving aside the history of coercive Communist secularization, first in the Soviet Union and then in the Soviet-dominated areas of Europe and Communist societies outside Europe. In Eastern Europe, coercive secularizing measures reached their peak in the 1950s. But both the success of these measures and the extent of religious revitalization following the collapse of Communism have been greatly influenced by the religious politics that preceded the Communist regimes. In this sense, these cases also fit the schema proposed here.

The three waves of secularization clearly require more precise definition. In fact, it may be misleading to refer to three waves of secularization, since the character of religious change in these different phases is sometimes so different that using the same term may seem inappropriate. We should also bear in mind that a wave is often followed by a massive countermovement; this may entail the revitalization of religion, the modernization of doctrine and/or organizational structures, and sometimes also a process of retraditionalization that makes it difficult to perceive the innovations involved.

The first wave

As far as the first wave is concerned, it is crucial that we get past the myth of the anti-religious French Revolution. Present-day scholarship is unanimous in acknowledging that in the early stages of the Revolution "no meeting could take place without invoking heaven, that every success had to be followed by a Te Deum, that any symbol which was adopted had be to blessed."[9] The ties between throne and altar had been severed but a new tie had been established—between Revolution and altar. During the first few years of the Revolution, attendance at church services appears to have increased rather than decreased. "The Festival of the Federation marking the anniversary of the Fall of the Bastille continued to be framed with religious ceremonial. Traditional Catholic feast days and processions were also widely celebrated in both Paris and the provinces, at least through the summer of 1793. Indeed, before that date, efforts by certain radicals to halt processions in Paris were roundly opposed by the population itself."[10]

Of course, this is not to deny that the French Revolution led to the "first state-sponsored assault on Christianity in Europe since the early Roman Empire."[11] But what prompted this escalation of the revolutionary process in an anti-Christian direction was not the religious but the economic and political role of the church. The first steps involved the total elimination of church taxes (the tithe) and of the church's seigniorial rights—and these measures were extremely popular. The next step entailed attempts to create a state church, in other words to nationalize the Catholic Church in order to ensure the political reliability of the clergy. These measures split both clergy and believers. The clergy were divided into those prepared to swear an oath of loyalty to the nation and those that saw this as a breach of their priestly vows. Those who refused to take the oath of loyalty found themselves confronted with the increasing and often deadly hostility of the revolutionaries, which reached fever pitch at times of war (from 1792 onwards) when such refractory clergy were accused of loyalty to the enemy (Austria). It was only when popular sentiment reached fever pitch at a near-millenarian moment in French history that "certain aggressively anti-religious or atheistic positions, positions advocated by a marginal fringe of 18th century philosophers and by a tiny minority of Parisian intellectuals early in the Revolution, acquired for a time a substantially larger following."[12] One of the tragic results of this spiral of hostility was papal condemnation of the Revolution and the principles it proclaimed, including human rights, as blasphemous, heretical, and schismatic. As early as 1856, in his book on the ancien régime, Alexis de Tocqueville made observations well suited to exploding the myth of the anti-religious French Revolution;[13] but this clashed with the religious politics of France in the late nineteenth century. My point here is that this process of escalation and polarization was largely contingent. But the history of France was lastingly influenced by it. A number of countries with deep religious and cultural affinities with France, such as Spain, Portugal, and parts of Italy were pulled into the same process of polarization, with consequences that are still being felt in present-day conflicts, particularly in Spain.

If, by way of comparison, we look at the Prussian history of the nineteenth century, we find that the decisive factor is clearly, not an imagined essence of Catholicism or Christianity, but rather the close alliance between political power and a monopoly religion. In the case of the failed revolution of 1848 in Prussia, we find a history, comparable in some respects with developments among French intellectuals prior to the Revolution, of disappointment and alienation among liberal and democratic revolutionaries vis-à-vis the Protestant state church, a church in which the territorial sovereign was at the same time *summus episcopus*, and that enjoyed tremendous financial and cultural privileges.

The second wave

In 1848, of course, the process of rapid urbanization and industrialization was already playing its own distinct and major role in religious change. As stated above, however, this was not a simple cause of secularization, but rather a challenge to the churches, which were confronted with new, unanticipated, sometimes unacknowledged and in any case uncontrolled social developments. In his magisterial studies of religion and the working class in Berlin, London, and New York, and on the fate of religion in general in the history of European and North American industrialization, Hugh McLeod has shown that initially this challenge was fundamentally logistical in nature.[14] When large numbers of people moved to the growing cities, they did not bring church buildings along with them; it was some time before the churches understood how important the infrastructural preconditions for religious life are. The methods of financing church construction also played an unfortunate role here. In

Berlin, despite considerable population growth in the last decades of the eighteenth century and in the early nineteenth century (until 1835), not one single new Protestant church was built. The total transformation of the structures of social inequality in an emerging capitalist industrial society highlighted the class character already inherent in religious life in new ways: poor city dwellers dared not go to church because they could not afford to comply with urban-bourgeois dress codes. The embourgeoisement of Christianity thus became a self-perpetuating process. The affinity of Protestant pastors for the growing nationalism of the period following the foundation of the German Empire in 1871, and their support for emerging German colonialism and imperialism, along with their hostility to the social democratic and trade union movement, alienated substantial portions of the male working classes from the Protestant church. Many of these workers developed a fervent belief in socialism in the sense of a secular political utopia, and in scientific-technological progress. Protestant women remained more committed to religious traditions and often dissuaded their menfolk from joining one of the church-leaving movements that sporadically arose, or from rejecting the church entirely—which to some extent masked the scale of the secularization that did occur. The churches in turn used the fear of social democracy, with its often aggressive hostility to religion, to present themselves to the state as indispensable, and they took active steps to counter this competitor.

These few remarks, focused on Prussia, cannot, of course, provide an adequate picture of the second wave. My intention is merely to highlight the change in a number of religiously relevant conditions of social life and point up the various fields of tension (the national, social, and democratic question; the gender dimension, and religious attitudes towards politics and other religions) in terms of their specific significance and interaction, while also taking account of how these constellations as a whole rested on the consequences of the first wave. Full reconstruction of such a genuine process of secularization would again remind us of the contingency of secularization. In the Ruhr area and in the Rhineland, the Catholic Church enjoyed far greater success in retaining the loyalty of the working class. Indeed, benefiting from clergy closely attuned to their communities, it managed to create a new, highly vibrant social milieu characterized by strong commitment to the church. When we admit the contingency of religious change, such alternative developments no longer appear as an exception to the rule of secularization, but as superior feats of institutional adaptation to changing conditions. The specific temporal structure here varies greatly from case to case; but there are identifiable, shared patterns of challenge and response in all these cases.

The third wave

The third wave, which occurred in the late 1960s and early 1970s, is once again a transnational European and indeed even extra-European phenomenon. Initially, the student movements of the time and other associated cultural and political movements and impulses often had Christian origins. The charismatic leader of the West German student movement, Rudi Dutschke, came from a deeply Protestant eastern German milieu— just as Mario Savio, the leader of the student movement in Berkeley, came from a deeply Catholic one. The Protestant student congregations in particular were crucial to the organizational infrastructure of the early student movement in the Federal Republic of Germany. It was not unusual for religious motives to inspire a political engagement that subsequently prompted conversion to secular convictions. But the reasons for such conversions and for the varying degrees to which this pattern applies in different countries are rather mysterious. Despite the transnational character of these movements, national conditions were quite specific. But one thing that all these movements had in common during this period, at least in Europe, is their highly secularizing impact. Significantly more than the two preceding waves, this wave led to a "normalization of the secular option" on every level of society and to a concomitant and subtle exoticization of believers. Why was this? If we try to answer this question sociologically then all the dimensions mentioned in explaining the first two waves retain their significance. But we must add another element. We may regard these social movements as guided by new values, new ideals, and new processes of sacralization, and not just as part of a "history of subtraction," to use Charles Taylor's term, that is, as attempts to rid oneself of something, to ease or destroy old restrictions. When these movements emerged in the 1960s, leading sociologists such as Talcott Parsons and his student the young Robert Bellah regarded them as harbingers of a new kind of religiosity or perhaps even a new religion, as the representatives of an "expressive revolution" *in* rather than *against* religion. This orientation towards the value of expressive self-realization, which emerged in the eighteenth century and was now embraced by large numbers of people, was new. Of course, the sociostructural preconditions for this orientation lay in such things as increased time in education and a general reduction in working hours. But it was not reducible to these factors and was soon linked with the new, anti-Puritan sacralization of the body and erotic love, a conception of sexual experiences as an intensive form of religious experience. Inevitably, this represented a tremendous challenge to religious traditions. This challenge itself found expression in a wide variety of ways: religious, areligious, and anti-religious. Of course, the nature of this expression depended partly on the reaction of the churches and religious communities to this challenge. The modes of religious expression included a new interest in Asian religious traditions, frequently with an emphasis on the erotic dimension (tantra), or a return to "good old basic paganism," to quote the Harvard psychologist turned drug guru Timothy Leary, after two millennia of the hegemony of the "Judeo-Christian power monolith, which has imposed guilty, inhibited, grim, anti-body, anti-life repression on Western civilization."[15] Responding adequately to this value change thus became a question of life and death for the churches. They could attempt to adapt to these "expressive values" in their teachings, practices, and organizational forms or, conversely, to conserve or even reinforce a pre- or anti-expressivist self-conception. These fronts are clearly apparent in, and lend a special intensity to, debates such as that on homosexuality.

From a sociological perspective, comparing Europe and the United States is a potentially productive way of analyzing the contingency of the secularizing effects of 1968. At present, two very different interpretations are in competition. One group of scholars regard the American movements of the 1960s as very similar to their European counterparts with respect to religion. On this view, the undeniable differences between (Western) Europe and the United States are not differences between these movements, but differences with respect to their hegemonic or nonhegemonic status in a particular national culture. The very hostile reaction of conservative religious milieus in the United States to the cultural upheavals of the 1960s is seen as the decisive factor in explaining why the United

States did not become far more secular even in the second half of the twentieth century. The alternative view is that the movements themselves were quite different. In Europe, so the argument goes, they were far more politically focused and geared towards the legacy of liberal and socialist secularism, while in America they were far more sensitive with respect to religion, which was in any case central to the civil rights movement; in America, these movements were even religiously innovative.[16] In any case, this question brings us to the self-understanding of the contemporary era, in the sense that the consequences of the third wave determine our present. To speculate, it may be that the tremendous increase in the public interest in religion in many Western countries over the past decade is a first indication that we might now have to reexamine and reevaluate the consequences of the third wave across a range of perspectives. This represents a challenge to nonbelievers because they must admit the contingency of this third wave. For believers and religious institutions, the challenge again lies in the need to acknowledge their own responsibility for this phase of secularization.

I believe that the dethroning of the secularization thesis represents much more than a minor modification of our understanding of "modernity" as such, as if we could erase this one component of "religious decline" from our understanding of modernity while leaving everything else intact. If there is no necessary connection between modernization and secularization, and if there are strong reasons to doubt other such necessary connections—such as those between modernization and democratization or between modernization and pacification[17]—then perhaps we must openly acknowledge that there is no uniform "process of modernization" at all and no uniform "modernity." Were we to do so, then study of the waves of secularization would be important to an adequate understanding of the present-day religious situation and would provide a model for investigation of the contingent processes of democratization and pacification as well.[18]

But I would like to conclude this chapter by addressing believers in a way I have already alluded to. The history of secularization should not be written in such a way as to suggest that atheistic ideologies came out of the blue one day to fall upon untouched religious communities. Leading Catholic thinkers of the twentieth century such as Max Scheler and key figures of Protestantism such as H. Richard Niebuhr and, taking things to the outer limits, Dietrich Bonhoeffer, already recognized that the history of secularization has always also been a history of the guilt of Christians and their refusal to take responsibility. Scheler, for example, responded to the previously inconceivable bloodletting of World War I with the insight that Christians could not simultaneously declare Europe deeply Christian while at the same time denying their responsibility for the war.[19] Perhaps, he mused, Christianity was still strong in Europe at the beginning of the twentieth century. In that case, it must have lost its focus on the Christian message of love and peace, given that it allowed or even encouraged this carnage. Or, he concluded, Christians must admit that Christianity had become weak because so many members of the working class, as well as the bourgeoisie, had lost faith in the churches, particularly over the course of the nineteenth century. Fascism and National Socialism and the far from heroic actions of most Christians during this period lend further credence to this alternative view. Of course, I do not mean to blame Christians for all the horrors that occurred and for their own persecution under totalitarian regimes. But Christians would do well to ponder how their own history is entangled in the various waves of secularization I have outlined here.

4

Modernization as a Culturally
Protestant Metanarrative

As the first three chapters have shown, beyond revision of the conventional secularization thesis, engagement with the history of secularization compels us to rethink our ideas of "modernization" and "modernity." It is not as if we might simply remove the secularization thesis, which asserts that secularization is a necessary part of modernization processes, from our ideas about modernization while retaining the rest in unchanged form. But if we set about this now inevitable task of rethinking fundamentals, it is useful to first recall the great extent to which ideas about modernization have always been pervaded by religious assumptions.

As far as Germany is concerned, the so-called cultural Protestantism of the nineteenth century is a particularly instructive case; in international terms, however, it is no exception. The "civil religion" of the United States, however much it might like to pose as independent of a specific confession or religion, was long deeply shaped by Protestantism, and much the same goes for the self-understanding of British colonialism. All three cases have exercised an impact on thinking about modernization far beyond directly political (or theological) contexts. In line with this, it is not just secularists who have shown an affinity for the secularization thesis. Protestantism too gave rise to a specific way of thinking in categories of religious progress that nourishes notions of modernization, and these notions retain their often unnoticed influence far beyond the revision of the conventional secularization thesis.

In this chapter, therefore, my first aim is to examine the extent to which we must view the idea of "modernization" itself as part of a culturally Protestant historical narrative. In the following chapter, I then subject the concept of modernity itself to scrutiny. I also indicate what an alternative conceptual framework might look like that better allows us to grasp the specific conditions of faith in the present era.

The cultural significance of Protestantism

"The cultural significance of Protestantism is undoubtedly a reality, but one that is extremely difficult to describe in the detail."[1] It was with this wise statement that Ernst Troeltsch began his brief essay on Protestantism and its relationship with culture in 1913 in the then current edition of the great encyclopedia *Religion in Geschichte und Gegenwart* (Religion in History and the Present). Here he distinguished between the consequences of Protestantism for European history as a whole and the development of a specifically Protestant culture. There were, he stated, three key aspects of general cultural significance: "the national cultures' gaining of independence, which now enjoys religious justification and consecration, the religious individualism of personal conviction, which is associated with a fundamental critique of convention, and the religious sanctification of this-worldly work."[2] Admittedly, this summary makes the Reformation's break with the world that brought it about appear more drastic than it was and than Troeltsch himself understood it to be. He was aware that "the gaining of independence by the national states and cultures . . . [was] long under way in any case, of course, as a result of medieval developments and . . . was proceeding apace regardless of the Reformation."[3] In this sense, what really mattered was only the dissolution of "Catholicism's status as unified world church," symbolized in the papacy. As far as religious individualism is concerned, the Reformers were not in favour of untrammelled freedom but envisaged an individualism based strictly on the Bible. This applies even to the free churches, which were opposed to the state churches and were often characterized by rigid orthodoxy or, at present, to tendencies towards "literalism" in U.S. Protestant fundamentalism. Troeltsch was far too skeptical about any "boundless" religious individualism in his day simply to identify it with Protestantism; instead, he thought in terms of an alliance between the religious elements of culture and modern individualism, whose roots in turn lie in very different spheres than those of Protestant culture. Troeltsch saw the third dimension of the general cultural significance of Protestantism in the "ensoulment of the system of natural professions with the Christian mentality of blessed faith in God and servient brotherly love, a process of ensoulment set in motion everywhere by the Christian obligation to love one's neighbor—in the shape of a professional commitment that sustains and fosters this phenomenon as a whole."[4] This is precisely the state of affairs that Charles Taylor has referred to in the past few years as the "affirmation of ordinary life," and for which he has found the wonderful phrase "God loveth adverbs" in the work of an English Puritan preacher (Joseph Hall): God "cares not how good, but how well."[5]

What is remarkable about Troeltsch's analysis is not just what he mentions but also what he does not consider worth mentioning. Certainly, the section that deals with the development of a specifically Protestant culture discusses the impact on family, state, economy, science, and art—but it is evident here that Troeltsch considers the continuities with pre-Reformation Christianity greater than the discontinuities. He mentions a religiously internalized patriarchalism in the family; reinforcement of the development, already under way, towards a bureaucratically governed absolutist state—reinforcement, because now the state had virtually been mandated to take care of the external dimension of the church system; and reservations about capitalist development within Lutheranism and Calvin's adaptation to the monetary and tax system in the city of Geneva. Troeltsch also mentions a great distance from science and, with a great sense of proportion, lists as achievements a very limited effect on art, chiefly in church music, religious poetry, and occasionally in church building.

Six theses on Protestantism

This sense of proportion is all the more impressive given that the historical and social scientific literature in Troeltsch's day, as it does to this day, teemed with strong theses about the crucial role of Protestantism in generating central phenomena of the modern world. There is rarely any of Max Weber's emotional ambivalence about these things, his melancholy-tragic perspective according to which Protestantism played a key role in producing a (capitalist) economic order that then largely deprived

Protestantism itself of room to breathe. Instead, this literature tends to be dominated by a seamlessly positive relationship to "modernity" and its achievements; with equally unreserved positivity, Protestantism is ascribed the role of driving force or pacesetter of this progress. While making no claims to completeness, I list six theses of this kind, characterizing each of them with reference to the work of one of their particularly influential exponents.

1. The "Jellinek thesis," first put forward in 1895 by the German legal historian Georg Jellinek (1851–1911), according to which the origin of human rights lies, not in the French Revolution and the spirit of the French Enlightenment, with its skepticism about religion, but in the struggle for religious freedom of North American Protestants such as Roger Williams.[6]

2. The most famous of these theses is, of course, the "Weber thesis," according to which "Calvinism, by applying its spirit of methodical and seamless industriousness to the field of capitalist production whose existence it facilitated, made an extremely important contribution to the emergence of the capitalist spirit, which values work for the sake of work."[7]

3. The thesis, proposed by the German historian Otto Hinze (1861–1940), that Calvinism was the decisive cause of the emergence of the modern bureaucratic state in the Netherlands and Prussia and that these in turn served as models for the rest of Europe, which I shall refer to as the "Hinze thesis."[8]

4. The thesis mentioned above on the connection between Protestantism and religious individualization, which we are justified in calling the "Troeltsch thesis" despite his reservations.[9]

5. The "Merton thesis," advanced by the American sociologist Robert K. Merton (1910–2003), according to which Puritanism provided crucial religious impetus to the rise of the modern natural sciences in England and Scotland.[10]

6. The thesis that modern democracy in the West is a product of Puritanism, which crops up most often in American rather than German intellectual history. We might name it after the American philosopher Ralph Barton Perry (1876–1957),[11] an expert on William James, who elaborated it in his work, or even call it the

"Dewey thesis," since John Dewey and his adherents are unquestionably among its exponents.

These theses, which are, of course, quite different, did not arise in isolation from one another. It is well known, for example, that as Max Weber acknowledged in his eulogy for his late friend Georg Jellinek, the "investigation of the scope of religious influences in general, even in areas where one would not expect to find them" in the latter's short book *Die Erklärung der Menschen- und Bürgerrechte* (1895; trans. as *The Declarations of the Rights of Man and of Citizens*) contributed to the development of the "Weber thesis."[12] Through their many years of friendship, collaboration, and cohabitation, Troeltsch's and Weber's perspectives became so closely entangled that it is almost impossible to disentangle the trajectories of influence and determine who came up with which idea first. Otto Hintze certainly found his thesis in embryonic form in the work of Gustav Schmoller, developing it further mainly through his research on the administrative history of Prussia and on the role of the (Calvinist) Brandenburg electors in Prussia's development as a state. But he was also one of the few historians of his time to take the emerging discipline of sociology and especially the writings of Weber (and Troeltsch) very seriously. The "Merton thesis" had already come into being earlier through application of the "Weber thesis," imported to the United States by Talcott Parsons, to the history of science—a field about which Weber said practically nothing, although it was clearly central to his ideas on Occidental rationalism. Finally, if I am correct, it was only after World War II that the "Dewey thesis" was combined with the "Weber thesis" in modernization theory— a far from self-evident development given Weber's skepticism about any affinity between capitalism and democracy.

No sooner had they been aired than all of these theses became caught up in interconfessional and national conflicts. Jellinek's text, for example, was perceived by French critics as a devious attempt to deny the French contribution to one of the most important modern achievements; as late as 1989, as if reluctant to impugn the French nation, Marcel Gauchet could write that it must be admitted that "German science" had established the influence of the American declarations.[13] In Germany, those eager to detach the issue of human rights from the constitutional traditions of the French "hereditary enemy," which were viewed with skepticism and resentment, greeted the "Jellinek thesis" with a sigh of relief. His text raised the hackles of Catholic critics, however, who vehemently disputed any Protestant claims to superiority with respect to the history of freedom and tolerance. Much the same applies to the reception of the other theses. The "Dewey thesis" is located very clearly in a political context in which, because of their international loyalty ("papism"), it was asserted that American Catholics could not be relied upon to prioritize the nation, and Catholic immigrants were perceived as a threat to democracy. In 1940, Sidney Hook, a student of Dewey's, described Catholicism as "the oldest and greatest totalitarian movement in history."[14]

Because each of these debates fired religious passions and, because of the fusion of religious and national identity, nationalist passions as well, in all of these cases, a whole slew of opinions has accumulated that makes it nearly impossible to produce a straightforward empirical account of the factual issues involved. It often seems that what we are dealing with here are not empirical questions about historical contexts, but mere conflicts of conviction—as if one were obliged to take a certain view as a Protestant or Catholic, Frenchman or American, and as if a positive attitude towards the values of democracy or human rights obligated one to ascribe credibility to one specific history of their emergence. As recently as 2008, in the debate on the constitutional lawyer Horst Dreier's eligibility for a seat on Germany's Federal Constitutional Court, one of the objections put forward was that he had disputed the Christian origin of human rights, despite the fact that Dreier, an active Protestant Christian as it happens, had merely expressed some objectively grounded reservations about any triumphalist Christian perspective. I would thus like to state openly at this point that in studying the facts, I have come to very different conclusions about the six theses. I do not claim to be entirely free of presuppositions or prejudices. But it seems to me that Jellinek was essentially correct, for example, while the "Weber thesis" seems very unlikely to find empirical confirmation.

It would obviously be beyond the scope of the present work to present detailed arguments about each of the six theses. I shall therefore restrict myself to just a few remarks on a number of them. In terms of the Americans' chronological priority and the idea that religious freedom for all produced the logical structure of human rights, it seems to me that the "Jellinek thesis" has been proved correct. It merely requires some modification with respect to the specific groups of religious agents involved and the trajectories of influence from the seventeenth to the eighteenth century and from North America to France. As far as the Weber thesis is concerned, its precise character has been contested for more than 100 years. If Weber did in fact initially associate it with causal claims, he largely retracted these in response to his contemporary critics. He came up with the notion of an "elective affinity" between the Puritan and capitalist spirit—but frankly I am still not quite sure what an "elective affinity" actually means in the context of economic history. From both ends of the spectrum researchers have gnawed away at the plausibility of Weber's construction. Believers do not appear to have experienced the Calvinist doctrine of predestination in the dramatic way imagined by Weber, and in terms of economic history the decisive turning point in the emergence of modern capitalism almost certainly occurred much later than Weber assumed. The "Weber thesis" thus plays no more than a marginal role in the writing of economic history; it is rather curious that the relevant text was canonized in sociology as a methodological exemplar. Weber's ideas are, in fact, irresistible as—aporetic—cultural analyses; unfortunately, many authors have also simplistically cited them as implying an economic superiority grounded in Protestantism. In analogy to "vulgar Marxism," we should probably refer here to "vulgar Weberianism." In other parts of his oeuvre, such as his great sociology of the city, Weber had more important things to say about the genesis of capitalism than in his essay on Protestantism. Over the past few decades, the Hintze thesis has been modified to take greater account of (Lutheran) Pietism. Some American historical sociologists have resisted this and placed greater emphasis than Hintze on the novelty of specific (bureaucratic) structures of rationality.[15] As far as the "Troeltsch thesis" is concerned, its originator was himself aware that the Reformation represented neither the origin nor the only source of processes of religious individualization; but he devoted very little space to the other sources in his writings. The "Merton thesis" plays a positive role vis-à-vis those visions of the history of science, which, anchored in a bastardized Enlightenment philosophy, portray the rise of modern natural science as the elimination of religious motives. Overall, however, it does little to explain the rise of the modern conception of nature. And at least since the election of the Catholic John F. Kennedy as president, the "Dewey thesis" has lost its political utility. It has in fact virtually disappeared because of the increased interest (e.g., on the part of J. G. A. Pocock, Quentin Skinner, and Philip Pettit) in the migration of republican thought from the Italian city-states via Britain to North America.

Each of these assessments is, of course, open to empirical contestation and may be questioned in light of new research. But the current state of the debate allows us to draw two general conclusions.

First, we should strive to avoid a misleadingly uniform concept of Protestantism that fails to do justice to the diversity of religious phenomena to which it refers.[16] As even so avid a Weberian as Rainer Lepsius concedes, Max Weber's *The Protestant Ethic and the Spirit of Capitalism* is, in fact, mistitled; it should really have referred to the "Puritan ethic." Weber ascribed to Lutheranism a transformative effect on the understanding of the professions, but no affinity with the emerging capitalism, let alone democracy. Against Jellinek, Troeltsch traced the struggle over religious freedom, not to the Calvinists, but to the "stepchildren of the Reformation," in other words the Baptists, Quakers, and a kind of free spirituality.[17] As far as the "Hintze thesis" is concerned, we have already referred to the roles of Calvinism and Pietism. We must add the important question of whether the Reformation received strong impetus from below in a particular territory, or was simply introduced from above. "Henry VIII was no Martin Luther,"[18] to quote John O'Malley's pithy remark, which applies beyond the borders of England. Finally, Troeltsch always made a sharp distinction between old and new Protestantism, ascribing an affinity with modernity only to the new Protestantism that emerged in the eighteenth century, whereas for him the "coercive ecclesiasticism of the national church" characteristic of old Protestantism represented a continuation of the medieval conception of a religiously defined cultural unity. For some, Troeltsch may have exaggerated these differences and underestimated Luther's innovations; but as an antidote to the tendency to iron out differences retrospectively, his remarks remain useful. Of course, in emphasizing the internal diversity of Protestantism, I am not telling historians of the Reformation or theologians anything new. But this point has often been neglected in the social scientific literature.

I shall briefly introduce the second conclusion of general significance by looking at the history of the "Weber thesis." If this thesis implies even the most modest assertion of causality, then we must ask why capitalist economic activity arose in all those places where the Protestant ethic had no impact. In line with this, in the 1950s, Talcott Parsons urged his young student Robert Bellah, with his fluent Japanese, to look for functional equivalents in the religious landscape of Japan that might explain the success of capitalism there (leading to Bellah's 1957 book *Tokugawa Religion*).[19] What Bellah found, however, went beyond the original question and led him to describe a trajectory of modernization characterized by particularist ties to the imperial family among all social elites and efficiency-oriented militaristic values. As capitalism gained traction in an increasing number of world regions, such as Confucianist China and South Korea and Catholic Latin America, the question at issue required further modification. Weber had presumed the existence of fundamental constraints in religious traditions, but it was becoming clear that religion was astonishingly adaptable. In theoretical terms, this is reflected in the reinterpretation of religious traditions in light of the requirements of capitalist economic activity; in practical terms, what we find are religious institutions and movements adapting structurally to those traits familiar from the history of Protestantism. These traits themselves may be, but are not necessarily, of a Protestant Christian character. Of course, once we see the flexibility of culture in the face of processes determined by other factors, it greatly diminishes the plausibility of any kind of cultural determinism. This does not mean that it is "capitalism" rather than culture that determines everything. Nothing could be less convincing than any sweeping, all-embracing concept of capitalism. The crucial point is that innovations may be deployed with very different functions in different situations. Wolfgang Reinhard has brought this out brilliantly with respect to the right to resist, popular sovereignty, and democracy. Regardless of their medieval precursors, these are often presented as Calvinist innovations, and contrasted with Catholicism as a religion of absolutism or with Lutheranism "as the doctrine of the subservient subject, which carries some of the blame for Germany's peculiar historical problems [*die deutsche Misere*]." Yet Reinhard shows how the modern right of resistance was "invented" by Lutherans in the mid-sixteenth century and propagated "until this was no longer necessary thanks to the legal protection provided by the Peace of Augsburg. By then it had 'migrated' to the Calvinists, who portrayed themselves as 'monarchomachs' [i.e., anti-monarchists, or republicans] amid the hardships of the French wars of religion, and especially after the St. Bartholomew's Day massacre, despite the fact that John Calvin's political doctrine was hardly less authoritarian than that of Luther and he would have liked nothing better than to have enforced his gospel with the help of kings and queens in the manner of a state church. When Henri of Navarre, admittedly raised as a Calvinist, became the most promising contender for the French crown, the Catholics suddenly turned into opponents of the monarchy, up to and including the theory and practice of tyrannicide, while the Calvinists, protected by the Edict of Nantes, very much like the German Lutherans before them, underwent a transformation into absolutists, until the tide turned once again due to the edict's revocation in the seventeenth century. In light of these facts, can we still claim that any group was on the way to modernity, or does this apply to all of them, or none of them?"[20]

Catholic reform: no unilinear modernization

At this point there is another step we must take if we are to prevent a historically untenable image of Protestantism from impairing social scientific theory building. We must take full account of the Catholic response to the Reformation. Those who believe wholeheartedly in Protestant myths of origin all too easily see Catholics as fervent defenders of pre-Reformation abuses. Unfortunately, and here we need only think of Carl Schmitt, there has never been any lack of Catholics who show little sign of religious experience but are full of admiration for the strong (or rigid) institutionalism of the Roman Church.[21] Protestants long conceived of the Catholic response to the Reformation in terms of the "Counter-Reformation." Here the Catholic response appeared as sheer and often violent repression, or otherwise as stagnation. Again, there was an interplay with those Catholics who asserted the church's unbroken continuity over time. But the fact that the term "Counter-Reformation" was coined not during the Reformation era itself but only in 1776, by a Lutheran legal historian in Göttingen (Johann Stephan Pütter), might give us pause for thought.

Not only was this term a new one, but the term "Reformation" itself had long been highly unstable and was by no means applied solely to Protestantism. Even the violent reestablishment of Catholicism in Lutheran territories was long referred to as the "Reformation of religion." It was above all in the late nineteenth-century *Kulturkampf*—Bismarck's suppression, with liberal support, of political Catholicism—that the term "Counter-Reformation" became popular, and it was from Germany that it spread around the world. It has virtually fallen out of use in serious historiography, although no similarly pithy alternative term has taken hold. Reference to "Tridentine," "baroque," or "early modern" Catholicism is of little help, and at the end of World War II, some suggested referring instead to "Catholic reform" or even the "Catholic Reformation." Certainly, the "counter- reformatory" aspects should not simply disappear, but it is crucial to recognize the great extent to which Catholic responses were more than just "rollback" efforts, and in fact represented a form of Catholic modernization and individualization. Francis de Sales's 1609 *Introduction to the Devout Life* is reminiscent of Joseph Hall's Puritan advice; as a new order, the Jesuits generated a new elite trained for activity in the world rather than specialists in otherworldly contemplation; the valorization of partnership in marriage was also more than a Protestant monopoly. These are just a few more or less random examples of the impressive research in this field over the past few decades; one could add many others. Ironically, we might consider internal Catholic reform one of the effects of the Reformation and thus demonstrate the culture-shaping significance of Protestantism with reference to Catholicism itself. But this is not the place for that project, nor can I provide detailed evidence of the many unremarked Protestant intellectual presuppositions at work in the writings of key sociological authors such as Max Weber.[22] All of this is of great interest, but it serves only further to undergird an argument that should have become plausible in light of the points already made. To put it in abstract terms, the important thing is to avoid presenting historical developments in such a way as to suggest that the old, from which the new has detached itself, continues to exist in the same way, and that the new is characterized only by this rupture. With respect to the topic of this book, this means that the self-renewal and global expansion of Catholicism are central to its history, and that when considering the history of Protestantism, we must not overlook the great extent to which it, too, practised religious suppression through an alliance with the state. Catholics suffered repression in Protestant territories. The worst examples are probably to be found in Irish history, where religious repression was practised both from outside and from above. Roger Williams, who was mentioned earlier in connection with the Jellinek thesis, ultimately had to leave Massachusetts and found the colony of Rhode Island in order to realize his vision of religious freedom—not just for his own confession but for all Christians, including Catholics, as well as for "Jews, heathens and Turks." To put it in more abstract terms, what matters is to deconstruct the notion of unilinear processes of modernization. I would like to briefly clarify this with reference to the most important sociological theorist of the early postwar period, Talcott Parsons.[23]

Right at the start of his long sociological history of Christianity, Parsons correctly notes that the processes of modernization brought about in part by the Protestant Reformation played themselves out "in complex interactions both with Catholic Europe and with the nonascetic, especially Lutheran, branches of Protestant Europe."[24] This is no doubt true, but like Weber's, Parsons's attempt to incorporate the further history of ascetic Protestantism is completely inadequate, because he ignores all retroactive effects—such as that of the Reformation on Catholicism and of modernization on Lutheranism, not to mention Christianity's impact on Jewish history. Here and in other contexts, when, for example, he underlines the continuity between Renaissance and Reformation,[25] or an affinity between Protestantism and religious tolerance,[26] he gives the impression of a unilinear process of cultural and social modernization in which, over the course of history, all the world's nonascetic Protestants, Catholics, Jews, and non-monotheists have lagged behind developmentally.

Other authors have extended this argumentational structure both forwards and backwards. Often, they regard the role of ritual practices as having been overcome and replaced, rather than supplemented and extended by the emergence of myth, while the role of myth is thought to have been supplanted by the emergence of theoretical reflection (as, for example, in Jürgen Habermas's relevant essays of the 1970s and in his truly radical notion of a "linguistification of the sacred" in his *Theory of Communicative Action*, originally published in German in 1981). The self-understanding of "Enlightenment believers" and Marxists exhibits the same structure, which is based on the notion of overcoming the old. But I believe that this structure was first developed in that form of Protestant self-understanding in which the Reformation is not viewed—as it was among the Reformers themselves—as the reestablishment of an unadulterated original Christianity, or as the consistent realization of a mission with which human beings are repeatedly challenged, but to which they repeatedly fail to rise. The crucial perspective here was, in fact, the one that portrayed the Reformation as a form of progress achieved once and for all, with only a few backward people failing to understand this advance and a few blinkered ones resisting it. It is because of this that I refer to the theory of modernization as a culturally Protestant metanarrative.[27] In the present era, the Parsons School (in the work of Robert Bellah and Shmuel Eisenstadt) has also generated a conceptual alternative to a notion originally grounded in this kind of Protestantism, one inherent but unnoticed in numerous aspects of social scientific ideas about "modernization." Bellah captures this in the phrase: "Nothing is ever lost."[28] What he has in mind here is an integration of levels of human behavior that differ in evolutionary terms—from the mimetic through the narrative to the theoretical—and thus the integration of forms of religious practice and symbolization. This is of great importance to an alternative to modernization theory that refuses to submit to an evolutionist conceptual schema.

But I would like to close this chapter by making a different point. In essays in the sociology of religion concerned with contemporary society, I have argued that what we are witnessing in present-day Germany is not just the erosion of confessional milieus but also the emergence of a new supraconfessional Christian life world, an idea that is backed up by data on marriage behavior and friendship relations.[29] Overcoming interconfessional polemics that taint our view of the Reformation and Protestantism as cultural resources seems to me crucial to the intellectual self-understanding of this newly emerging milieu.

This makes the research briefly assessed above of great importance—not just to social scientific theory building but also to ecumenical understanding.

5

The Age of Contingency

The social sciences have no choice but to try to help meet the need for analysis of the contemporary world, a need that makes its presence felt in the public sphere primarily in association with crises and processes of rapid change. Many professional sociologists regard every attempt to capture the reality of the present in this way as frivolous. The greater the claim to professionalism, the more strongly such views tend to be held. It is easy to see why. Scientists are trained to proceed as cautiously as possible when collecting empirical data and testing hypotheses that explain phenomena, but also when scrutinizing theoretical arguments and constructing comprehensive explanatory frameworks. This means that there is a gap in their self-understanding between knowledge gained in a methodical manner that remains aware of its limits—in other words, the style of thought that they represent—and rash generalizations, empirically shaky assertions, and moral or political discourse of the kind that dominates in the public sphere. The question, of course, is how to deal responsibly with this gap between methodologically secured knowledge and the public need for pithy interpretations of the contemporary world. If the professional social sciences simply leave the public sphere to those brave—or unscrupulous—enough to disregard the limits of methodologically secured knowledge, then the latter will get all the media attention and will be the only ones to influence citizens' political attitudes. This is undesirable in itself, but is also likely to widen the gap described above.

Two basic types of contemporary
analysis of the modern world

It seems to me that present-day analyses of the modern world are
dominated by two basic types. I call the first "monothematic analyses"
and the second "explanations of epochal rupture." The first type gained
traction when the term "late capitalism" began to lose plausibility in the
late 1970s. It became increasingly clear that the capitalist economy was
gaining new momentum, and that unprecedented technological progress—particularly in information and communication technology—was
more of a danger to the "actually existing" socialist societies than it was
to the capitalist ones. Ulrich Beck's concept of the "risk society" (*Risiko-
gesellschaft*),[1] which in light of the Chernobyl disaster seemed compelling
to many when it was advanced in 1986, is the best known of these new
analyses. Beck's sensational success encouraged a large number of scholars to emulate him and put forward similar analyses. Gerhard Schulze
came closest to achieving the same kind of success with his "experience
society" (*Erlebnisgesellschaft*) theory, put forward in 1992; in contrast to
Beck, however, his impact was mainly limited to Germany. "Knowledge
society," "communication society," "multi-optional society," "responsibility society," "network society," "decision society"—these are the key terms
in some of these analyses. A journalist has now compiled several volumes
containing condensed versions of these monothematic analyses in light of
the question "Which society are we living in?" This inevitably creates the
impression that contemporary readers, eager to enhance their understanding of the world, have no option but to choose between a dozen or more
such analyses, each one-sided in its own way, and implies that these are an
embodiment of sociology. I believe that there are valuable cores to all of
these concepts, but it would be a big mistake to think we must "choose"
between them. What we need is an integration of these analyses or, better still, a multiperspectival analysis that allows us to integrate the rational
core of each of them.

The second type of analysis typically involves the claim that an era is
coming to an end before our eyes, and that we are witnessing the beginning
of a new one. At times this is already implied in the monothematic analyses. For Ulrich Beck, the rise of the risk society entails the devalorization

of all classical sociological concepts such as class and family and the idea of a value-free science. Some of these authors limit themselves more clearly than Beck to the end of one component of society (examples being the "post-military society" and perhaps also the "post-secular society"). The most intense debate was that on the shift to so-called postmodernity, in which it remained chronically unclear whether we were dealing just with a change in cultural currents or also with a new era in terms of social structure. Again, I have no wish to dispute that many of these "post-" analyses have a foundation in reality. In my opinion, this applies most to the concepts of "postindustrial society" as presented in various forms in the work of Alain Touraine and Daniel Bell, who emphasize the increased role of the service sector, education, and science. But the ceaseless flow of analyses asserting epochal rupture ends up tiring the public. In much the same way as in art before World War I, when new styles and "isms" (fauvism, cubism, etc.) succeeded one another in rapid succession, there is initially an increase in public attention, since, of course, no one wants to feel out of touch with the world they live in and simply ignore the historical rupture proclaimed by others. But the inflation of such declarations soon exhausts people's interest as they become skeptical of the artificial, desperate quality of what seems like mere attention seeking. It is impossible to believe that every year sees the beginning of a new era. Among the historically educated, it is a venerable truism that it is only much later that we can know whether an event was truly "historic." This second type of analysis, then, requires a greater balance between continuity and discontinuity.

This balance and multidimensionality are two of the criteria that a social scientific analysis of the contemporary world ought to fulfil if it wishes to avoid detaching itself from the theoretical and empirical findings of the social sciences and from an awareness of history. My suggestion is that the best way to achieve this is by reflecting anew on the concept of contingency. To be more precise, I believe we need to rework our conception of modernity and modernization through a new sensitivity to contingency. In what follows I would first like to clarify what exactly I mean by this programmatic statement. I then go on to demonstrate, at least in outline, two kinds of outcome of this reworked conception. At issue here are, first, the understanding of social change, and, second, the reasons why, in my opinion, the contemporary era may be referred to as an "era of contingency."

In the decades immediately following World War II, the social sciences were dominated by two major theoretical paradigms, both of which informed research and analysis of the contemporary world: modernization theory and Marxism. There was stiff competition between the two, but it is undeniable in retrospect that they also had significant characteristics in common. The most striking example is probably the assumption of a "tight coupling" between the various societal spheres and developments within them. Certainly, modernization theorists accused Marxism, with its notion of base and superstructure, of espousing an empirically untenable economic determinism that resulted in the neglect of other drivers of social change. But modernization theorists immediately abandoned the multidimensionality to which they thus implicitly laid claim in the sense that the prevailing functionalist framework suggested that unavoidable adaptations in other societal spheres, such as the economy, can be inferred from cultural changes. The risk here was of countering a trite economic determinism with an equally trite cultural one. Modernization theory is even more open to criticism with respect to the second criterion, namely, the need to strike a balance between continuity and discontinuity. Typical modernization theorists—although not Talcott Parsons himself—have assumed a dichotomous rupture between premodern, so-called traditional societies and modern ones.[2] The history of modern societies is then portrayed as more or less "continuous" and progressive. Wars, violent regimes, and genocides are explained as exceptions and "special paths"; the collapse of "antimodern" movements and regimes is viewed as guaranteed. Even pessimistic alternatives to the historical optimism of modernization theory and Marxism—most clearly in the "dialectic of Enlightenment" espoused by Horkheimer and Adorno—remain beholden to the unilinearity of this historical perspective: they too emphasize the dialectical character of a single process of the increasing domination of nature, but fail to distance themselves from the idea of a single process of modernization. And if a third stage is added to the two dichotomous stages proposed by modernization theory, such as "post-modernity," or a "reflexive" or "second" modernity, we find that the relevant authors often attempt to characterize the present era by putting forward the very assertions—concerning the end of all traditions and fixed ties for example—already applied by conventional modernization theory to the beginning of modernity.

Against the fetishization of "modernity"

My thesis is that we can only escape this labyrinth of competing analyses, all of which nonetheless assume a homogeneous modernity and a total rupture between it and preceding history, if we break with what the Canadian political scientist Bernard Yack calls "the fetishism of modernities" in a 1997 book of that title.[3] Yack builds on Herbert Schnädelbach's critical interpretation of the "dialectic of Enlightenment" and refers to the fetishization of modernity in all those cases in which a multitude of heterogeneous social processes and phenomena are totalized into one grand object called modernity. For him, the result of this homogenizing conceptual operation is a "social myth," namely, the myth of one single modernity and one single process of modernization.

My aim is to roll back this homogenizing process of mythologization. In fact, I assert that there is no uniform process of modernization featuring tightly coupled subprocesses. We should instead view the supposed subprocesses of modernization as relatively independent ones, although there are causal relationships between them. We can then examine the exact degree of their independence from one another, their differing temporal structures, the tensions between them, and their potential for integration individually and without functionalist presuppositions. In attempting to understand the relationship between these processes in this way, we find an alternative to the "tight coupling" and functionalist assumptions of totality in the concept of "contingency."[4]

Of course, we should not cease to fetishize modernity only to fetishize and essentialize these subprocesses. These too are no more than conceptual abstractions. If, for example, we refer to secularization as one such (supposed) subprocess of modernization and then distinguish the various phases or waves of this secularization over the course of history, we must always remain aware that the events that occurred during these various phases may have been very different from one another. By using a homogenizing concept, we merely impose a false sense of uniformity upon them. As Max Weber and the American pragmatists already knew, the only antidote to this danger is a consistent action-theoretical approach. This turns our attention to the actions that give rise to social processes and social orders, and through which these are realized. But this also throws up the question of the extent to which these processes are in fact produced by actors' intentions and to what extent actors experience historical processes as undetermined and amenable to influence. This is the second context in which the concept of contingency takes on force. In other words, what interests me here is whether we can characterize the present era by underlining the increase in individual action options and how the awareness of historical contingency has developed. If we look at these various components together, we find that a theory of contingency is the macrosociological counterpart of a creativity-oriented theory of action.[5]

First, though, I would like to focus on the revision of our understanding of modernity and modernization in light of contingency. Two ways of thinking prevent many authors from attaining such a contingency-sensitive understanding. These may be understood as a legacy of Marxism and modernization theory. I believe it is a legacy of Marxism to imagine that the "master trend" of modernization is a process of "economization," that is, the ever-greater penetration of the economy, but of other spheres of social life as well, by the logic of rational utility calculation. The idea that the "master trend" is an ever-advancing process of functional differentiation is, I would suggest, the legacy of modernization theory. This is clearly not the place to cut these two assumptions down to size through detailed analysis.[6]

Economization or functional differentiation?

As far as the thesis of economization is concerned, the first point to note is that the true founders and classical figures of modern economic thought, such as Adam Smith, did not expound this idea. The famous debates on the relationship between economic theory and moral philosophy in the work of Smith would never have occurred if he had assumed that all spheres of human life were soon to be penetrated by the logic of economic thought. In fact, the first radical exponent of this idea was Karl Marx; the classic text in which it was developed is the *Communist Manifesto*. This not only features the famous analysis of the development of the capitalist world market, the constant increase in economic productivity, rapid efficiency gains in transportation and communication, and the sensational growth of urban settlements, but above all the notion that "all that is solid melts into air." Marx predicts that the nation-state, family, professions and religion will all soon disappear, as will every social class other than the bourgeoisie and proletariat.

These predictions or prophecies have not just been proved wrong. It would be fair to say that most of the phenomena whose decline Marx declared a foregone conclusion were, in fact, yet to enter their golden age. This applies to the nation-state in Europe, but especially in the rest of the world; it also applies to the family and the importance of professional qualifications. And the prediction of the disappearance of religion was crude Eurocentrism. We need only compare Europe to the United States, where, in both absolute and relative terms, the nineteenth century was an age of dramatically growing religious communities ("the churching of America"). The fact that Marx's predictions failed so dramatically, however, has not stopped many participants in present-day debates on globalization from making the same kind of statements about an imagined process of economization that sweeps all before it—although generally devoid of the historical framework and thus the utopian hopes that lent credence to the paean to economic transformation found in the work of Marx and Engels. Richard Rorty, for example, described Marx as a precocious critic of globalization, as if he had erred with respect to the timing of his predictions but, precisely because of this, had been especially prescient.[7] It seems more plausible to me that the factors that originally led to the failure of these predictions are likely to scupper them once again. What we need to do is challenge the assumption of an inexorably advancing process of economization both by exploring possible "civilizing" effects of the market and by analyzing the complex institutional preconditions of long-term economic dynamics.

With respect to the thesis of economization, Marxism's great competitor, the theory of functional differentiation, has the advantage of having no need to assume the spread of a logic of action throughout every sphere of society. It allows for complementarities and compensatory processes. When the (Marxist) historian Eric Hobsbawm studied the bourgeois family in the nineteenth century, he called it "the most mysterious institution of the age," because it seemed to him inexplicable why "a society dedicated to an economy of profit-making competitive enterprise, to the efforts of the isolated individual, to equality of rights and opportunities and freedom, [should] rest on an institution which so totally denied all of these."[8] Theorists of differentiation will find nothing mysterious here. For them it is obvious that the disciplining of actors, with all their passions, a process that has turned them into rational, interest-focused agents in the economic sphere,[9] makes it very likely that nonprofessional life will become pervaded with passions and a longing for emotional intensity.

There is absolutely no compelling reason to assume that a value will take hold in every sphere of society and displace all other values. If we follow Stephen Toulmin's important book *Cosmopolis*,[10] the Cartesian notion of a rational method of solving philosophical problems was not the product of a culture in which the value of rationality held uncontested sway. In fact, it was the product of desperate hopes for a route out of the seemingly irresolvable, politically charged confessional conflicts of the early modern age. The institutionalization of a partly neutralized sphere of the political and the concomitant privatization of the religious are often explained in a similar way. What we are dealing with here, then, are complex institutional constellations, divisions of labor and balances of power. Theorists of differentiation explain all of this far better than the thesis of economization. Of course, their ideas may also be overstated to the point of meaninglessness. If I may make so bold, it seems to me that this is what happened in the work of Niklas Luhmann, when he conceived of subsystems as hermetically sealed universes each with its own code, rather than exploring their constant mutual interpenetration and their embedding in a horizon of values. But the plausibility of the theory of functional differentiation is not due solely to its substantial descriptive capacity, but also to normative factors. In the work of the leading American exponent of this school of thought (in my generation), Jeffrey Alexander, the influence of Michael Walzer, who differentiated the value of justice in accordance with different social spheres, has played a decisive role. And it was central to the "conversion" to differentiation theory of leading European left-wing social theorists, such as Jürgen Habermas and Alain Touraine, that they saw this theory as a means of resisting new moves towards totalitarianism.

So while the descriptive capacity and normative appeal of the vocabulary of differentiation should not be underestimated, its explanatory power is weak. This is often overlooked. As a rule, differentiation theory fails to shed any light on the causes of functional differentiation, its various forms and varying extent in different societies and eras; it also struggles to deal with actors, countervailing forces and to specify the duration of the processes that are assumed to occur. This already applied in the nineteenth century when William James penned his inimitable caricature of the application of elements of biological theory to the social sciences in the work of Herbert Spencer: "Evolution is a change from a non-howish, untalkaboutable, all-alikeness to a somehowish and in general talkaboutable not-allalikeness by continuous stick-to-getherations and something-elsifications."[11] Durkheim and Simmel avoided a bombastic jargon of differentiation through an ascetic limitation to the quantitative dimensions of group size and density, as did Talcott Parsons by viewing differentiation as just one of four dimensions of social change. But all of this was lost again in modernization theory and in the work of Luhmann. Again, I am unable to put forward detailed arguments here.[12] My aim is to show that neither "economization" nor "differentiation" can provide us with the golden key to understanding "modernization."

As I have indicated, my alternative suggestion is not to explain the supposed subprocesses of modernization in light of a single causal dimension, but to view them in terms of their contingent relationships with one another. Of the classical figures of social theory, it seems to me that Jakob Burckhardt—one of the few thinkers of the time, by the way, who did not espouse the theory of secularization—went furthest in this direction in his *Reflections on History*. Burckhardt distinguishes between the "three powers" of state, religion and culture before going on to develop his reflections, in strictly combinatory fashion, in accordance with the "six conditionalities": culture as conditioned by state and religion, the state as conditioned by religion and culture, and religion as conditioned by state and culture.[13] This theoretical design itself thwarts any assumption of a "master trend." Among contemporary sociologists, it seems to me that conflict theorist Randall Collins has come closest to this when—in discussing, as it happens, the supposed German *Sonderweg*, or special path—he subdivides the concept of modernization into four distinct processes (economization, bureaucratization, democratization, and secularization).[14] I myself would like to add to this list, which I find very useful, the social psychological process of individualization and the intersocietal dimension of advancing pacification.

The first benefit of this approach is a heuristic one. It furnishes us with a "tableau idéologique," a schema that allows us to classify and survey analyses of the contemporary world and macrohistorical theses. We discern, for example, the major role played by "bureaucratization" in Max Weber's understanding of modernity and the minor role it played for Emile Durkheim. For Weber, the pacification of international relations was an outlandish idea, but not for Durkheim. Simmel focused on the interplay of economization and individualization. In this way we can identify one-sided elements and omissions in classical and contemporary analyses of the contemporary world. Far more important than this metatheoretical utility, however, is the fact that we also recognize the actual variability of constellations, which vanishes in the pseudo-homogeneous concept of modernization or is marginalized in attempts to identify special paths or identify deviations from the "correct" path. In the context of the present book, this relates mainly to the conditional nature of secularization processes. The refutation of the thesis that modernization, through a kind of inherent necessity, leads to secularization (in the sense of the decreasing importance of religion), to which the first chapter was dedicated, can build on empirical arguments and on a theoretical critique of secularization theorists' conception of religion. Conversely, however, it also throws up the question of how processes of economization, democratization, and individualization—to name but a few—impact on society in such a way as to result in secularization. The refutation of the thesis of secularization, after all, does not mean the denial of instances of actual secularization. For example, the thesis put forward by "religious economists," that free competition among the purveyors of religion increases religious vitality, is then viewed as an inherently plausible but again one-sided explanatory hypothesis, in other words, one that disregards legal and political conditions. Only the systematic analysis of the "conditionalities" can do justice to the idea of a contingent relation between "subprocesses."

What is contingency?

This assertion is of relevance to analyses of the contemporary world in the sense that it alters our understanding of modernity, but it by no means applies only to the present. Why then do I refer to our present as an age of contingency? The reason is that the concept of contingency seems to me better able than any other to convey both the massive increase in individual action options and the growing number of experiences that result from this massive increase. As examples of these increasing possibilities, we need only think of the options available to us when choosing a partner or the way in which we are confronted with a plurality of religions, worldviews, and ways of life. Equally, technological developments enhance individual mobility and opportunities to communicate with those physically absent and enlarge the capacity for both intervention and self-determination in spheres (such as biological reproduction) that were regarded as indisposable until recently. I do not claim that this objectively verifiable increase in options applies to every member of society to the same degree, or that everyone experiences it as an increase in their capacity for action. Action options are affected to a particularly great degree by social inequality, and this also applies to opportunities to develop the capacity to see options as opportunities in the first place, rather than as dangerous or as difficult to cope with. Those who feel disoriented may long for fewer options and may even seek aggressively to eliminate options. What we need here are not global statements but precise descriptions, each of which can, of course, only claim a limited degree of validity. I myself have focused on the field of religion, in other words, on the effects of constant confrontation with religious-ideological plurality on the emergence of intensive commitments of value and belief.[15]

It will surely help us to define the term "contingency" at this point. The tendency has taken hold to refer to those things that are neither necessary nor impossible as "contingent," in other words those things that pertain but do not pertain of necessity. The greatest danger in adequately understanding this concept is the tendency to equate it with the concept of the "random." I have come across this notion again and again in the remarks of those who have misunderstood my ideas. In fact, a theory of the random would be a highly implausible project; the thesis that everything is random is very unlikely to advance understanding. The roots of this misunderstanding lie in the fact that the term "contingency" is also used as an antonym of necessity—like that of the random. But the meaning of an antonym depends greatly on the meaning of that with which it is antonymous. When, as in premodern philosophy, necessity was understood as a well-ordered cosmos, then contingency, as set out by Ernst Troeltsch in his brilliant essay of 1910, referred both to the incomplete and imperfect character of the merely sensory-material world, as well as to the free and creative character of God's interventions in the world.[16] A dramatic semantic change occurred when the modern scientific revolution replaced the image of a well-ordered cosmos with that of a causally determined universe, governed like clockwork by the laws of nature. This new view made it impossible to find metaphysical certainty and repose in contemplation of the well-ordered cosmos or a pious faith in a nature established by the Creator God in accordance with his unfathomable will. As a result, retaining the old ambiguity, "contingency" took on the meaning of "randomness" but also that of "free will." The search for certainty migrated from the ontological to the epistemological level: Descartes's belief in the possibility of a method guaranteeing certain knowledge is the clearest expression of this. Ever since the so-called saddle period around 1800, with its radical temporalization of human self-understanding, there have been repeated waves of insight into the contingency of human existence, along with ever-new means of suppressing contingency, such as teleological or evolutionist philosophies of history.

I am not concerned here with the minutiae of the history of ideas,[17] however, but with the ability of this concept to enrich analyses of the contemporary world. The concept both sensitizes us to the increase in our action options and to the randomness of what we go through in our lives, a randomness that arises in large part from the increase in individual action options. Increased action options produce new forms and requirements of social life. The old duality in the concept of contingency—"randomness" and "free will"—thus appears once again, although now the concept no longer refers to the action of the Creator or idealized free individual, but to all human beings and their coexistence. With respect to both meanings, we must distinguish between objective attributability and subjective experience. Increased action options may be experienced as a form of redemptive liberation, but also as a burdensome requirement to make decisions; the wealth of experiences produced by others' freedom may be experienced as an increase in intensity but also as threatening.

The increase in individual action options may also give rise to paradoxical problems that end up restricting individuals' de facto action options. The traffic jam is such a striking symbol of the problems of present-day sociation because it illustrates so vividly how the aggregate of individual decisions may lead to a collective phenomenon that radically restricts individual options. The older literature on the topic of contingency—such as John Dewey's important book *The Quest for Certainty* of 1929[18]—articulated hopes of the scientific-technological mastery of contingency, but it is the antithetical emphasis on the paradoxical consequences of increased options that has gained the upper hand in the more recent literature on the topic—for example, in the work of Niklas Luhmann. From this perspective, all hopes of a form of collective action that protects individual room for maneuver and prevents paradoxical consequences are declared hopelessly obsolete. This gives rise to the idea, also paradoxical, that everything is becoming more contingent, but nothing can be changed because the logic of functional differentiation and of the functional subsystems will always hold sway, no matter what.

In the field of religion, of course, we are dealing with a different kind of paradox, not well conveyed by the model of the traffic jam. Many thinkers have linked religion with the fact of the indisposable element in human existence. One of the last remaining exponents of the idea that modernization necessarily leads to secularization—the American political scientist Ronald Inglehart, an expert on value change—explains secularization in light of the decrease in existential risks as a result of the increasing prosperity generated by modernization.[19] For him, increased life expectancy as a result of medical and economic progress is crucial, because the risk of one's own death or serious illness has been reduced and it is also less common to experience the loss of loved ones. Inglehart calls this the "existential insecurity hypothesis." He differs from conventional theorists of secularization only in the sense that he includes the demographic dimension of social change. For him, while modernization necessarily leads to secularization, the world is becoming increasingly religious, since modernization also leads to lower population growth or even demographic contraction. To overstate things slightly, this means that the secularized nations are, as it were, dying out. It is, of course, very one-sided to associate religion only with alarming and tragic forms of contingency, while ignoring enthusiasm and a sense of gratitude, mercy, and grace. It is also short-sighted to imagine that the degree of contingency is pregiven and independent of interpretation, rather than seeing that we require sensitivity to the suffering of others in order to recognize this suffering as requiring interpretation in the first place. In debates on religion and contingency the questions at issue include whether we should understand religion exclusively—to cite a frequent misunderstanding of the work of Hermann Lübbe—as the practice of coping with contingency; whether—as Peter Berger asserts—the development of fixed value ties is rendered completely impossible under conditions of high contingency; and whether—as Richard Rorty assumes—in contexts of contingency, all fixed norms and values evaporate, and a fathomless relativism holds sway. My answers to these questions are different from those mentioned above. For me, faith does not represent a technique for coping with contingency, but is the precondition for a specific approach to contingency; I would argue that under conditions of high contingency, there may well be stable commitments to individuals and values, but the nature of these commitments changes; and a sensitivity to contingency does not produce relativism but "contingent certainty," which entails an awareness of the contingency of its emergence.

In analyzing the contemporary era, we must link the reconstruction of the concept of modernity with the action-theoretical reflections set out above, both of which are grouped around the topic of contingency. With respect to the topic of religion, what this means in concrete terms is that at present, under conditions of high contingency, the development of religious commitments is occurring in an intellectual environment in which people are ceasing to believe that secularization is a necessary component of modernization. This, it seems to me, is the core determinant of the present-day religious situation in our society. But on a very fundamental level, the processing of experiences of contingency always takes place against the background of a specific cultural awareness of contingency. The intense experience of contingency in situations such as wars may prompt individuals to abandon constructions of history that disregard contingency; but such intense experiences may also *increase* the need for such constructions. I derive my description of the present era as an age of contingency from the perception that today, generally speaking, the increase in individual action options can no longer be processed through an interpretation in the style of old philosophy-of-history metanarratives, but only through a new narrative that understands itself in light of contingent certainty.

In my view, it is only in this context that we can understand why a book as empirically unsubstantiated and philosophically lax as Jean-François Lyotard's *La condition postmoderne* (1979) could make such a strong impression on contemporaries.[20] What Lyotard did, in a highly subjective way, was sublimate his own disappointed rejection of Marxism and left-wing radicalism into a comprehensive thesis of the end of all metanarratives. His tone was euphoric rather than tragic: finally liberated from the constraints of transhistorical progressive ideologies, we were now free to embrace heterogeneity and the present. It is easy to warn of the dangers of rashly generalizing from an individual tale of political disillusionment, and to note that declaring the end of all metanarratives constitutes a (new) metanarrative in itself. Yet the social fact is that many people recognized themselves in Lyotard's analysis. It is true that the teleological and evolutionist intellectual schemas (Marxism and modernization theory), which had been revived in the decades after World War II, collapsed again in the 1970s, increasing the appeal of the contingency-sensitive theories that had already been developed around 1900. This made Lyotard's text a main source for slogans of public discourse at the time. We can only avoid his logical self-contradiction if we eschew the idea that this shift is a final victory and treat it instead as contingent and thus always at risk. The break with teleological and evolutionist conceptual schemas does not, after all, excuse us from narrating a comprehensive history and relating it to the genesis and fate of our ideals.

6

Increased Options as a Danger?

The question mark in the title of this chapter is there for a reason: our next step is to get to grips with warnings about the dangers of increased options. Many commentators, after all, refer to these increased options as dangerous rather than beneficial to individuals. Many jeremiads have appeared bemoaning advancing fragmentation, the loss of values in our time, the disappearance of community, trust, ties and character-building—and of faith. These lamentations constitute their own rhetorical genre of cultural criticism and social scientific analysis of the contemporary world. There are basically conservative and basically progressive variants. The existence of such a genre should make us cautious about the schematizations and narrative constraints it imposes on its exponents. It is in this more general framework that we must examine what faith as an "option" actually means.

When the American historian Thomas Bender once attempted to find out when exactly in American history, according to the scholarly literature, individualism and materialism triumphed over the ideals of Puritan community life, he discovered that this claim has been made for every historical period from 1650 on. He finally asked in exasperation, "How many times can community collapse in America?"[1] In a very similar way, we can now ask when precisely the alleged contemporary fragmentation of our society began—and if we are really doing justice to contemporary changes if we forever force them into the schema of decline and loss. With reference to one of the most influential recent sociological analyses of the present era, I shall first explain the problem with these interpretations in more detail. I then sketch out an alternative interpretive approach that enables me to make a number of observations about the contemporary state of faith.

The decline of character

The "influential analysis" I have in mind is Richard Sennett's book *The Corrosion of Character: The Personal Consequences of Work in the New Capitalism*, whose title clearly indicates its location in the genre of analyses of decline. Sennett sets out to describe a process of corrosion, of degradation or subversion. But what, according to Sennett, is undergoing such corrosion in our day? It is people's character—and what he means by this is the long-term molding of personality, particularly its emotional dimension. This character, he writes "is expressed by loyalty and mutual commitment, or through the pursuit of long-term goals, or by the practice of delayed gratifications for the sake of a future end."[2] According to Sennett, however, today such character formation is fundamentally at risk from an epoch-making shift towards a new type of capitalism, which he calls "flexible capitalism": "How can long-term goals be pursued in an economy devoted to the short-term? How can mutual loyalties and commitments be sustained in institutions which are constantly breaking apart or continually being redesigned? . . . How do we decide what is of lasting value in ourselves in a society which is impatient, which focuses on the immediate moment?"[3] While early sociology and classical Marxism described the destructive effects of industrial capitalism on preindustrial communities, Sennett is responding to the dissolution of social, economic, and political structures that set in, at the earliest, during the New Deal era in the 1930s, but that really took off only after World War II in both the United States and Europe. The contrastive foil here, then, is an era of enduring prosperity, a working world largely bureaucratized by the welfare state and the juridification of labor relations, the golden age of the nuclear family and institutionally backed biographical stability. There is tremendous irony here. When this regime existed, it was sharply attacked by left-wing critics because they constantly measured it against an idealized socialism. Now it is retrospectively romanticized almost as much as the preindustrial world was by early sociologists. Sennett has his hands full attempting to counter the tendency towards romanticization evident in his text—to some extent against his will—and to distance himself from what is ultimately the obvious interpretation, namely, that he wants to retain, if not return to, a "deadening politics of seniority and time entitlements."[4] But despite these avowals of an orientation to the present and the future, the theme of decline ultimately predominates in his book. Job security, he insists, is a thing of the past, and the same applies to the possibility of relying on the qualifications one has attained, of taking one's lead from fixed and clearly recognizable rules in the working world, of planning a life for oneself and one's children. Bonds to one's work colleagues and loyalty to the firm cannot, we are told, arise in this way. Age and experience are systematically disregarded, since only youth is associated with flexibility; age is equated with rigidity. Length of service as such no longer means anything. For Sennett, new structures such as flexible working hours, increased individual responsibility in the workplace, dehierarchization and teamwork are characterized by a degrading superficiality of social relations and the subtle masking of genuine power relations. Traditionally, commentators on human alienation under capitalism cited the routine character of bureaucratic work and the repetitive handling of small components in assembly-line production, but these suddenly appear far more benign. The new flexibility is by no means regarded as a step towards greater creative self-realization, but as the elimination of the opportunities for freedom opened up by routinizable activities. The rapidity and self-certainty with which these conclusions were drawn demonstrate that they are based, not so much on empirical investigation, as on preexisting intellectual compulsions. And Sennett's empirical basis is, in fact, extremely sparse. That his assertions are generally taken at face value is surely due to their affinity with the expectations of mainstream cultural criticism.

The simplest and most obvious question we can ask about Sennett's findings is surely how comprehensive the change he claims to have occurred in fact is. Sennett assumes that companies' self-presentation reflects their social reality. But as we all know, it is a far from easy task to transform such things as the postal service, or national rail operator—from a bureaucracy or "benefits office with railway attached"—into a customer- and market-oriented service-sector enterprise. So it is at the very

least precipitate to paint a totalistic picture of trends towards flexibilization. More important than the question of how new and how flexible this
new flexible capitalism might really be is to examine the tacit assumptions
that Sennett makes when he extrapolates the long-term consequences of
observed changes. And he makes a whole number of such tacit, but by
no means self-evident, assumptions. He assumes that strong ties emerge
only where there is enduring cohesion. He assumes that the lack of stable
career patterns leads to the experience of disjointed time. He asserts that
in the American suburbs, friendship and local community are only fleeting in character. He is unable to see that the capacity for distantiation
might mean more than just keeping your distance. And he believes that
only very few people, in fact, not many more than the vanishingly small
elite who participate in world economic forums, whom he wittily refers
to as "homo davosiensis," might be among the winners of flexibilization.
All these assumptions, however, are very questionable empirically and,
furthermore, logically problematic. Empirically, they are contradicted by
a wealth of findings that have repeatedly demonstrated individuals' and
social structures' adaptability to greater flexibility. But far more important than relativizing Sennett's work from an empirical standpoint is to
uncover the logic at work in his analysis—particularly since it is present
not just in his work but also in other well-known analyses that together
make up a cartel-like web of cross-references. The parallel with Ulrich
Beck's descriptions of the dissolution of traditional socio-moral milieus in
Germany is unmistakable. But Beck is more ambiguous. He uses the term
"individualization" for this change in forms of social integration partly
in the sense of individuals' increased decision-making autonomy, and
partly in the sense of an anomic loss of orientation, of singularization and
destabilization. In his work, whether this development is evaluated as an
opportunity or danger depends on the context, although he never sets out
exactly what makes individualization one or the other. In terms of reception, however, it is once again the pessimistic voices that predominate.
Yet we should never forget that as late as the 1960s, when the dissolution
of the classical confessional and workers' milieus set in, the pillarization
of German society was rightly regarded as an obstacle to a functioning
democracy, and this process of change was therefore greeted with a sigh
of relief.[5] The work of both Beck and the German sociologist Wilhelm

Heitmeyer, who does research on conflict and violence, feature the notion that right-wing extremism and juvenile violence itself are the result of individualization and disintegration. Rather than being a malevolent caricature, the following is a direct quotation from Heitmeyer himself: "The more freedom there is, the less equality; the less equality there is, the more competition; the more competition there is, the less solidarity; the less solidarity there is, the more isolation; the more isolation there is, the less social integration; and the less social integration there is, the greater the degree of ruthless self-assertion."[6] I think Heitmeyer is wrong about every single one of the steps in this six-stage and apparently seamless causal chain supposedly leading from the market to violence. This causal schema does justice neither to the Anglo-Saxon societies nor to the author's own findings on the propensity for violence, a fact to which he implicitly responds by constantly attempting to finesse the definition of the term "disintegration." Heitmeyer's work also features verbal qualifications, but again in such a way that the central message remains unchanged. And this is that capitalism results in disintegration, which results in right-wing extremism and violence. And the new capitalism, the flexibility-oriented and debureaucratized variety, seems to lead to these consequences to an even greater extent than the old form.

What is the logical problem with this construction, which seems plausible to so many people? It seems obvious but is nonetheless too simple to say that we must understand every change not just as a danger but also as an opportunity. To assert this would be to engage in the same kind of platitudinous attempt to immunize one's ideas made by the authors mentioned above. Certainly, this thoughtless cultural pessimism loses a good deal of its plausibility if the two-stage schema of order and disintegration is replaced by a three-stage one that leaves room for reintegration through individuals' creative action and goes on to ask under what conditions creative adaptation succeeds or fails. So far, every new technology has prompted diagnoses of decline that appear mere curiosities in retrospect. But I am not concerned here with the opposition between cultural pessimism and civilizational optimism, with the painting of rosy pictures as an antidote to doom-mongering, with downplaying problems as a way of opposing cultural criticism. Instead, I suggest we make a sharp distinction between the problems of social integration and those of increased contingency. It is the concept of increased contingency, rather than fragmentation, disintegration, or corrosion of character that seems to me best-suited to conveying the transformed conditions that now hold sway for the development of commitments to other individuals or values.

As set out in more detail in the preceding chapter, this concept sensitizes us both to the increase in our action options and to the happenstance nature of what we go through in our lives, which is in fact due in substantial part to this increase in individual action options.

An alternative view: increasing action options

Let us look at a concrete illustration of this. Every city magazine now features wistful appeals to turn a chance encounter into something more along the lines of: "Café Lutz, Sunday 4 Nov. 1pm, Goltzstraße. Looking for woman with straight black hair sitting at table with friend. Can't get you out of my head." The well-read may be aware that this ad from the Berlin city magazine *Zitty* was expressed in more elevated literary form more than 150 years ago by Charles Baudelaire—in his poem "À une passante" (as translated by William Aggeler):

"To a Passer-By"

The street about me roared with a deafening sound.
Tall, slender, in heavy mourning, majestic grief,
A woman passed, with a glittering hand
Raising, swinging the hem and flounces of her skirt;
. . . .

A lightning flash . . . then night! Fleeting beauty
By whose glance I was suddenly reborn,
Will I see you no more before eternity?

Elsewhere, far, far from here! too late! *never* perhaps!
For I know not where you fled, you know not where I go,
O you whom I would have loved, O you who knew it!
[Ô toi que j'eusse aimée, ô toi qui le savais!]

The *Zitty* ad and Baudelaire's poem relate to an event with which everyone who lives in a big city is familiar, and on which the early sociological literature on the peculiar features of life in cities placed great emphasis: the multitude of surprising encounters and the sudden proximity to unknown others. City-dwellers are so accustomed to the fact of this momentary closeness that they no longer perceive it as such; they become inured to it and develop a repertoire of looks and behaviors that enable them to deal with situations of anonymous proximity. But these experiences differ from sudden encounters with wild animals or robbers in the preindustrial forest. Now we continuously encounter others for whom we ourselves constitute a source of surprise in the same way that they do for us. It is only because we are able to choose with whom we make contact, and also because we assume that others can choose as well, that fleeting eye contact in the Café Lutz or on a Paris boulevard can trigger the fantasy—and perhaps even the realization—of the love of our lives. Behind the accumulation of random experiences that are part and parcel of the complexity of a large city, then, there lies a real increase in action options, in this case with respect to choice of partner.

In Baudelaire's poem, of course, this experience is articulated as a tragic one. Just as lovers who met through a chance encounter tend to endow it with a predetermined quality, to imagine that their lives had led them inexorably to that point, Baudelaire is certain that the passer-by would have been his great love—but also that he will never meet her again. In a momentary epiphany, he could merely catch a glimpse of this love before it vanished from view. In the twentieth century, it was above all World War I that turned the awareness of contingency into a mass phenomenon—often with tragic overtones.[7] What matters here in the first instance is the increase in individuals' action options—as we encounter them at present most strikingly in the bioethical debate. We are gaining the potential to intervene in biological reproduction far beyond improved contraceptive options and prenatal diagnostics. It is not yet clear precisely how our values relate to this potential. As my example from life in the big city was intended to show, increased action options produce new forms and requirements of social life.

New opportunities for commitment

What does this contemporary change mean for the potential to develop commitments to values or people? If it is true, as I claimed in my book *The Genesis of Values*,[8] that our value commitments do not arise from rational-argumentational justifications, but from experiences of self-formation and self-transcendence, in other words from experiences that push us beyond ourselves and make us feel that what we have experienced is "good" with a sense of subjective self-evidence and affective intensity—if this is correct, then our first conclusion must be that the mere knowledge of values or individuals never generates commitment. This insight also allows us to conclude that the rational knowledge of a range of alternatives does not unsettle our existing commitments. To put it in drastic terms, the mere awareness that there are billions of other women on the planet does not shatter my commitment to my wife. The mere confrontation with the fact that in addition to the Christian religion, there are other religions or secular worldviews does not shatter my commitment to Christianity. Increased contingency as such does not imperil the development of commitments. But it does influence the nature of the commitments capable of surviving under these conditions. It is this that compels us to look for forms of commitment to other individuals and values that are commensurate with contingency.

Today all of us are familiar with contingency-adapted forms of commitment to lovers and children. The dissolution of fixed gender and generational roles and forms of the domestic division of labor that used to appear self-evident has by no means plunged people—as the logic of analyses of decline would suggest—into constant fear and behavioral insecurity, although these certainly occur. What has changed in a broad range of ways is how partners interact with one another and with their children. American sociologists were trying to capture this as early as 1945 when they referred to a shift "from institution to companionship" (in the words of Ernest Burgess).[9] The effort involved in coordination and discussion increases, and individuals become more sensitive to the nature of a given situation and to others' needs. These abilities and communicative acts compensate for the loss of "static" stability and potentially generate a more elevated, "dynamic" form of stability.

We should be thinking in similar terms when it comes to the field of value commitments. Value commitments are changing in three ways in order to remain possible under conditions of high contingency. These are proceduralization, value generalization, and empathy. The first form (proceduralization) is immediately comprehensible if we generalize and transfer to everyday life the principles central to the self-conception of the liberal-democratic, constitutional state. In significant part, of course, these principles developed out of the insight that major differences in worldview and interests can neither be repressed nor eliminated in a future utopia; if we wish to deal with them peacefully our only option is to recognize them. In terms of law but also in terms of political participation, this presupposes agreement on procedures and a willingness to stick to them even if the outcome clashes with one's own aspirations. This generalized willingness to obey the law, to be tolerant, and to embrace fairness and pluralism, shows that proceduralization is by no means value-free. But it shifts possible dissent from the jointly recognized level of difference to a meta-level; deviations from the procedural rules can and must remain subject to moralization, but the moralization of presupposed differences has to be overcome. In a certain sense, this proceduralization leaves value commitments untouched; it merely requires people to consent to joint procedures.

The picture is very different with respect to "value generalization"— a concept I borrow from Talcott Parsons's theory of social change.[10] What he had in mind here are developmental processes in which differing, particularist value traditions develop a more general and for the most part more abstract understanding of what they have in common. An example would be the Christian-Buddhist dialogue on loving one's neighbor and compassion, or on human rights and human dignity. While it is true that certain values may be regarded as products of a particular cultural tradition, in this case human rights as an outcome of the Judeo-Christian tradition, other traditions may very well be reinterpreted in light of this value or, better, they can reinterpret themselves in such a way as to bring out their own potential to articulate the same value. But this presupposes that such reinterpretation is not detached from the affective underpinning of a given tradition. Value generalization, then, means neither neutralizing proceduralization nor an inevitably ineffective process of intellectualization of specific, binding value and belief systems, but rather a recognition of the ground shared by different value traditions that leaves their particular binding force untouched. In contrast to the false divisions in the fraught debate on liberalism and communitarianism, I do not view proceduralization and value generalization as alternatives but as involving different fields of application. A contingency-adapted value commitment depends on both, on complying with procedures that bracket off value differences and on coming to terms with other value traditions in such a way that we may be prompted to reinterpret and modify our own value-based self-conception.

And it is important to stress that both of these require "empathy," a term that has now become almost fashionable. What we are seeing here is in fact the unacknowledged return of the German term *Einfühlung*, translated into English from around 1900 as "empathy." It refers to the ability to see the world through others' eyes. If it is true that conditions of increased contingency require us to encounter a growing number of others, whose otherness cannot be tranquilized through clear-cut classifications, then this capacity for empathy will be increasingly important to peaceful coexistence. People who only know their own world will think it is the only one there is. Oscar Wilde called this the "dogmatism of the untravelled."

So increased contingency does not render value commitment impossible but changes the way in which it is rooted in individuals. Proceduralization, value generalization, and empathy all demand a capacity for reflexive distancing from oneself, for flexible internalization and creative articulation. But the capacity for reflexive distancing should by no means be misconstrued, as in Sennett's work, as coldness, and flexible internalization does not mean feeble internalization with reservations. It would be more appropriate to acknowledge the greater degree of freedom in such a commitment—and this also applies to the new forms of commitment to individuals. Under conditions of high contingency, we cannot act without such freedom in commitment, which balances the strength of the commitment with the awareness of its contingency, and in this sense always requires us to renew our consent to existing commitments. Under these conditions, individuals are continuously confronted with situations in which they themselves have to make up their own minds about what to do. Further, this scope for individual decision-making and collective interpretation necessarily and increasingly confronts us with alternatives. Contra Sennett, who treats flexibilization as a calamity afflicting hapless individuals, I would take seriously the experience of organizations based on voluntary membership. Increasingly, only those that give their members a chance to define and organize their core mission will have any prospect of attracting new members or engaging existing ones. So the question is to what extent the change in working structures has been caused by employees' demands rather than merely by the supply of jobs. In Sennett's work, flexible working-time regulations are criticized both as a merely apparent increase in freedom and as "unequally apportioned and strictly rationed."[11] Sennett is unable to resolve this duality, which is illogical in this form, in his frame of reference.

Of course, this is not to deny that people are sometimes stretched to breaking point. Crises of orientation, enduring confusion, and indignation may stunt the capacity for judgment or even lead to the aggressive elimination of options. Our task, then, is to locate the problem zones in the development of contingency-appropriate value commitments and work out how we might enhance the transmission of values. Unfortunately, at present we have very little secure knowledge about the first of these issues. This is probably because sociologists' research is geared too much to the schema of disintegration and because much of the research in developmental psychology on morality has a cognitivist-rationalist bias; such research has long tended to neglect the motivation for morality and an orientation towards ideals rather than norms. One apparently obvious assumption is that we can expect opportunities to adapt to contingency to vary mainly in line with educational level. The hypothesis here is that the more educated people are, the more they demand flexibility and the better they deal with it. But I am far from sure that this hypothesis really makes sense. This quickly becomes clear if we look at empathy. Empathy is not something people have independent of motivation or a particular field of application. Those who are entirely unwilling to put themselves in others' shoes will not develop effective empathy—assuming they have the capacity for it in the first place. In thrall to ideologies, even educated people often dehumanize entire categories of their fellow human beings, refusing to treat them with sensitivity. Less harmfully, the flipside of Wilde's "dogmatism of the untravelled" is the blasé attitude of those who have been everywhere but are no longer "learning" anything. The motivation to empathize may prompt us to make the effort to understand, but this is an effort we have to make again and again. Soberingly, while it is probably even more common for people to attribute superior empathy to themselves than above-average intelligence—and both probably increase with the level of education—the actual efficacy of empathy is likely to be associated with motivations fuelled by substantive values and preexisting tensions in their lives, as well as with the level of education. Without the acquisition of specific values that enjoin people to perceive moral feelings for others, attempts to educate them in empathy will remain hollow. Even practice in procedures of a legal or participatory nature always risks lapsing into the mere calculation of interests if there are no values motivating people to perceive these procedures themselves as valuable. In line with this, the three forms of value-orientation consonant with contingency that I have identified do not lie entirely on the same logical level, since both empathy and proceduralization ultimately depend on value generalization.[12]

So far I have touched only marginally on religious faith in this chapter. But it is obvious that the conditions for transmitting (or rediscovering) faith are also very much affected by the tendency towards increased options. Many analyses of the contemporary world highlight increased options but tend to have nothing to say about their consequences for faith.[13] Conversely, researchers specializing in religion use many terms that assume that contemporary believers simply construct an eclectic mix from the available options: à la carte, patchwork, pick-and-choose.[14] As a result, so the argument goes, their faith is inward-looking and fails to challenge them to transform themselves. The most popular of the many analyses is that of Peter Berger. According to him, the growing pluralism of religious options is very likely to lead to something he calls "cognitive contamination," in other words, a blending of religious ideas, values, and lifestyles. His work here is shaped by the psychological assumption that the encounter with other values and worldviews compels people to acknowledge, initially just a little but then with increasing intensity, that their own ideas and attachments are only apparently self-evident. This almost inevitably—Berger thinks—gives rise to a relativism for which all these values and worldviews are somehow equally good or equally unjustifiable. For Berger, then, faith as an option means that faith is purely subjective and unstable. But such a faith can develop no resistance to those forces of secularization that are due to other causes. These forces also promote pluralization, which results in the dynamism of Western secularization.

Even facts that at first sight appear to contradict this analysis, such as the new emergence and spread of religious fundamentalisms, are explained as psychological responses to trends towards relativism.[15]

In other places I have tried to thoroughly refute Berger's construction by presenting historical, sociological, and philosophical objections.[16] In many cases, after all, religious pluralism—in the society of the United States, for example—has strengthened rather than weakened faith. Flexible internalization is not a weaker or more superficial internalization. Pluralism may itself be perceived as a value in which people believe with profound conviction.

In his great work *A Secular Age*, Charles Taylor agrees with my critique of Berger and makes it clear that, for him, increased options and growing pluralism do not give rise to relativism and secularization; but they do result in "fragilization." What Taylor means is that because of the growing number of options, people more easily "convert" from one religious community to another, or, we might add, from the state of faith to nonfaith or perhaps from nonfaith to faith. But in no way does this inevitably mean that the faith ultimately adopted (or retained) is less intensive, as Berger appears to assume. On the contrary, the faith that emerges from this precarious contemporary situation may be all the stronger because it has been directly compared with an undistorted alternative.[17] Again, it may be worth our while casting a comparative glance at the situation with respect to personal attachments. The fact that it is easier to find alternative partners or spouses is likely to lead to a statistical increase in the probability of divorce; but it does not consistently reduce the quality of marital ties; in many cases it enhances it.

We should thus be on our guard against rash cultural critiques that posit increased options and pluralism as the main factors hampering the transmission of faith. The relevant analyses here rightly draw attention to the danger of eclecticism or "Don Juanism" (Paul Ricœur) in the field of religion, but they are wrong to portray this danger as inevitable. Such analyses fail to grasp how little our certainty about our commitments to persons, values, or religions is affected by insights into the contingency of their genesis. We live in a condition of contingent certainty. Because such analyses fail to grasp this, their exponents are quick to abandon hope of turning the option they recommend into a living option.[18] Individuals do not experience all available options as livable, as truly appealing to them, even in a potential sense. The vibrancy of an option depends on the abilities of those who espouse it and show the way by living it, and on their confidence that, even under present-day conditions, rather than preserving a weak little plant in need of protection, they are championing an option whose appeal—if correctly understood—is virtually irresistible.

Religious Diversity and
the Pluralist Society

Whenever participants in contemporary debates—which are often heated—refer to the clash of civilizations and the prospects for global peace, or to social cohesion and the factors threatening it, the topic of religion is not far away. This is not surprising: religions, after all, present values in a vivid form, while believers gain motivation and action orientations from their faith and place themselves in traditions that they also seek to pass on to their children, students, or political supporters. When we take a closer look, however, we soon come up against a number of difficulties.

Like other religious communities, despite all their efforts to impart values or foster reconciliation, the Christian churches are by no means unanimously thrilled when social problems or international conflicts prompt others to task the churches with the engendering of social cohesion. They are then prone to feel degraded to the status of mere tools or functional systems in society and resist this instrumentalization of faith. Faith, they object, and this applies to attempts to resolve international tensions through interreligious dialogue as well, is not the result of the rational conviction that it is of utility to individuals, other people, society, or international peace.

Conversely, some warn against regarding religions as possible sources of social cohesion in the first place. Religions, they argue, are necessarily particular entities underpinned by particular communities. On this view, then, quite regardless of their character, religions have an inherent divisive potential that must be tamed by state and society and bridged by religiously neutralized institutions.

The following reflections are a modest attempt to sketch out a realistic approach to interreligious understanding and religiously grounded value transmission at a time when the various religions are coming into increasingly close contact through migration and globalization, while (particularly in Europe) the Christian tradition has been forced on the defensive and has to some extent even been marginalized by various forms of secularization.

Understanding religions

Our point of departure here must be the insight that religions are more than value systems as normally understood.[1] Those who believe certainly do not view their faith primarily as a logically consistent system of propositions about the good—let alone as mere emotionally tinged morality. Religious faith is based on intensive experiences; it makes participation in rituals possible, which are in turn sources of experiences; it offers role models that invite us to learn from them, and it contains stories and myths that guide us in interpreting our own lives and history and help us answer questions about the meaning of our existence. The crucial point here is that all these experiences, symbolizations, and narratives are far too rich to be captured in simple formulas. Rather than reducing religions to value systems or to systems of religious statements, then, it makes more sense to extend our enquiry into experiential foundations, symbols, and narrative structures to include all nonreligious value systems. Certainly, believers derive orientations from their faith; but this happens, not through an abstract process of logical derivation, but through concrete interpretation of ever-risky situations of decision-making and action.

This insight into the character of religions—but to some extent also the character of temporally stable and widely effective secular interpretations of the world—must therefore come first. It enables us to understand an effect that is frequently felt, but that many see as paradoxical, when we attempt to provide an overview of the world's religions or competing value systems. If religions, whether in the school classroom or in academic discourse, are presented as mere systems of values or of religious propositions that believers take to be true, then for the most part the initial effect is one of confusion, then indifference. Even if the intention of such accounts was to help participants make their own selections in the market of interpretive options, religions presented in this way inevitably seem difficult to understand; they strain the limits of comprehensibility and in some ways seem like mere curiosities. And this applies in such accounts not just to the religions of "exotic" cultures, but even to those that have deeply molded the recipients' culture in the past; even these religions prompt many to shake their heads in wonder at their ancestors' irrationality. As a rule, nonbelievers find confirmation here of their default assumption that it is best to keep one's distance from the peculiarities of religious life. If mere distance is not enough, their only other option is to try to adopt an objectivizing perspective on religions in all their diversity, in other words to comprehend them as the consequence of economic, political, or social conditions or classify them as a psychological, and perhaps even biological, aspect of human life.

For believers, there are fundamentally two possible ways of dealing with such confrontation with the diversity of religions (and secular interpretations of the world). Like self-certain secular thinkers, they, too, may attribute truth and perhaps even self-evidence exclusively to their own faith; in this case, for them, too, other religions become a mere cabinet of curiosities—"mumbo-jumbo," as some missionaries described the religions they found in their missionary areas. Other missionaries, in contrast, developed a sympathetic and sometimes even admiring approach to the religions they encountered. They viewed them as impressive interpretations of authentic experiences, undergone by individuals in other times and cultures, both in their everyday life and in their interaction with the divine. Looked at in this way, the self-revelation of God is inherent in many or all religions.

So it is a prerequisite for such a productive relationship to religions to view them neither as value systems nor quasi-scientific doctrinal systems but as attempts to interpret human experiences. On this view, secular and religious approaches are distinguished by the fact that the former consider everything encountered through human experience as occurring solely in people's minds, while the latter believe it is possible to have a genuine encounter with the divine, through the experiences of self-transcendence of both believers and nonbelievers; in other words, they assume that we have the potential to experience genuine transcendence. The flip side of a productive curiosity about religious interpretations of the world is a certain humility with respect to one's own interpretive background. This background too then becomes recognizable as the expression of constitutive experiences—which in turn implies that even our own interpretation of experiences of self-transcendence should be regarded as never entirely successful, never entirely exhausting the wealth of experience. This is all the more important if these experiences are viewed as a genuine encounter with the transcendence of the divine, which can only ever be revealed apperceptively through the words and symbols of human beings, but can never exist for us in itself. From this perspective, the Word of God, as set out in holy scriptures, is not the unmediated self-expression of God, but the transmission of God's intended message in the recipients' frame of reference. This means it is always imparted by specific, historically and culturally situated individuals, in other words within the limits of their knowledge and imagination.

On this view, we can only prevent an engagement with religions from inspiring confusion and indifference if this engagement includes an open-minded attitude towards the other and humility about our own beliefs. It is, of course, easy to call for open-mindedness and declare our willingness to embrace it. But noncommittal open-mindedness results in nothing more extensive than the search for common ground, the attainment of the lowest common denominator. It does not open us up to anything truly new, and cannot, therefore, lead to any change in our own world. In this sense, open-mindedness is merely a minimal condition that must apply if we are to engage in any more strenuous process. But a serious engagement with religions is a strenuous process that challenges our own certainties. As with the understanding of other people or cultures in general, a comparison with the acquisition of foreign languages is helpful at this point. When we learn a foreign language it increases our sensitivity to the contingencies of our own language; we see that the semantic structures or syntactical rules of our language are not necessary as such, are not demanded by structures inherent in the world. It takes time and effort to acquire every additional language. The attempt to learn several languages at the same time may succeed; but it may also confuse us and we may get nowhere with any of them. A comparative course on the grammars of the world's languages may offer us information of various kinds, but will certainly not teach us how to use any particular language—and the same goes for attempts to gain an overview of religions. Certainly, acquiring additional foreign languages seems to be easier for people who have learned a number of them; but there is no truly generalized language-learning ability to spare us from having to acquire a given language.

Stages of interreligious dialogue

George Santayana captured this in the famous formula: "The attempt to speak without speaking any particular language is not more hopeless than the attempt to have a religion that shall be no religion in particular."[2] Frequently, then, in a Christian context, as soon as individuals wish to go beyond the mere transmission of their own religious tradition, the "realistic" approach that I aim to sketch out here often begins with ecumenical dialogue. The opportunities and difficulties of intra-Christian ecumenical dialogue may serve as an initial training before we go on to promote communication between religions in a broader sense. Ecumenical dialogue can, in fact, help overcome differences that are more apparent than real, and help us discover whether these relate to theological doctrines or merely to stereotypes of others' mentalities of the kind that have been passed down from history, or that continuously reappear, because different confessions feel the need to mark their boundaries with others and emphasize their own distinctiveness. But it may also endow us with a sobering awareness that often not even the differences among the Christian confessions are described in a common language, so that one side's proposal to identify common ground may be perceived by the other side as a mere strategy of encroachment. Ecumenical dialogue in Germany is simplified by the fact that it encompasses only a small segment of the Christian spectrum. Orthodox and Oriental forms of Christianity play only a very negligible role in this spectrum and the Protestant segment is essentially devoid of the fundamentalist currents that are so important in the United States, and of Pentecostalism, whose rapid spread in parts of Latin America and Africa has been nothing less than spectacular.

In the second half of the twentieth century, the most substantial addition to ecumenical dialogue has been Jewish-Christian dialogue. Racist anti-Semitism and above all the murder of millions of Jews by the Nazis have confronted the Christian churches with the unavoidable task of thinking afresh about the traditions of Christian anti-Judaism and facing up to their own guilt and responsibility with respect to the Holocaust. The term "Judeo-Christian tradition," which now trips so easily off the tongues of Christians, did itself not become widely used until the twentieth century; this is often forgotten. This term is itself an expression of the laudable attempt to overcome the tendency of some Christians to emphasize the differences between Christianity on the one hand and a distorted image of Judaism on the other. Yet even if it is free of any subtle implication that Judaism is merely a preliminary stage on the path to true faith, some Jews may perceive even this seemingly unproblematic hyphenated term as an attempt at absorption. Drawing on a Polish literary quotation from the nineteenth century, Pope John Paul II sought to map a route out of this conundrum by referring to the Jews as "elder brothers in faith." Building on the work of the Jewish religious thinkers Franz Rosenzweig and Martin Buber, the former Protestant bishop Wolfgang Huber refers to "two ways of faith" that only come together from an eschatological perspective.[3] Christianity simply cannot exist without dialogue with Judaism.

As yet, neither ecumenical nor Judeo-Christian dialogue has achieved its ultimate goal. Nonetheless, at the beginning of the twenty-first century, it is plain that we must pursue another project of the greatest importance—what we might refer to as dialogue among the Abrahamic religions, in other words Judeo-Christian-Muslim dialogue. Present-day attempts to politicize Islam may lead to an Islamophobia that does no justice to this great religion and may even transfer to Islam stereotypes drawn from Christian anti-Judaism. It goes without saying that distorted anti-Jewish and anti-Christian beliefs held by Muslims are just as dangerous. Rémi Brague is surely right to insist that a dialogue between these religions, whose history is characterized by a range of intensive interactions—influence and hostility—should not seek to smooth away the profound differences between them through any intellectual laziness. Such dialogue presupposes that we "understand others as they understand themselves, grasp the meaning of words as they use them, and accept an initial situation of disunity in an attempt to achieve greater understanding against this background."[4] If we do this, it quickly becomes clear that it is not enough to see secure common ground in references to a holy book or Abraham or monotheism, since even the status of the book and the genealogy and the conception of God differ tremendously. On the theological level, it seems to me that the Christian doctrine of the triune God occupies a central place in this dialogue. What may appear like a relapse into polytheism from a Jewish or Muslim perspective should prompt Christians to reflect on the depth of their own conception of God. Islam, which, of course, always understood itself in part as the overcoming and critique of Christianity, and accused Christians of distorting the true message of Jesus, requires dialogue with Christians just as much as Christians require dialogue with Jews. Christianity needs to explore how it is perceived by Islam in order to correct its own self-perception.

While the current political priority of "Abrahamic dialogue" seems indisputable, the next great task is already apparent: dialogue between the Abrahamic religions and the various forms of South and East Asian religiosity. Like other efforts to achieve mutual understanding mentioned here, this dialogue too has already begun, the first moves being made by the nineteenth century at the latest. Very often, however, this has not really been a dialogue with the representatives of Buddhism itself, for example, but with European or American experts, converts, or contemporaries who have merely flirted with the idea of abandoning the Jewish-Christian-Muslim tradition and thus the monotheistic frame of reference itself. This is going to change, not just because of the growing economic and political significance of Asia, migration and the politicization of Hinduism (in India), and even to some extent of Buddhism (in Sri Lanka and Myanmar), but also because of the considerable appeal of these religions in the West, particularly Buddhism. In his speculations on an impending "era of adjustment,"[5] Max Scheler anticipated this necessity as early as 1927. Neither vague references to the merits of Asian mysticism as an alternative to monotheistic faiths nor sweeping claims that the mystical traditions of Jews, Christians, or Muslims have always included anything we might learn from Asia are of any use here. Again, the only productive approach is a willingness to genuinely confront the other without disowning one's own heritage.

Opportunities and obligations

My thesis, then, is that today the only way to transmit faith in a manner in keeping with the modern world is to face up to this task of dialogue, but far from bracketing off our own religious tradition, we should regard it as a vital prerequisite for any productive confrontation with the other. There are two obvious objections to this thesis. Some will assert that religions are mutually exclusive. For them, the perspective I have sketched out here of multilevel, arduous dialogue would simply be illusionary; far more probable, they would argue, is a conflict between religions, which, if it becomes politicized, will inevitably trigger a clash of civilizations. Others will object that, at least in the radically secularized parts of Europe, we cannot assume that people will be in a position to build on their own traditions; multilevel interreligious dialogue would fall at the first hurdle, and all we can do, however disadvantageous this may be, is seek to obtain a neutral overview of the diversity of worldviews and religions.

I shall briefly respond to both these criticisms. The first is based on a fundamentally mistaken premise, namely, that religions or cultures are capable of action. My remarks, in contrast, work on the assumption that it is always only human beings who take action, in other words, individuals and their associations, organizations, and institutions.[6] These human beings believe and disseminate their beliefs, they have experiences and interpret them, they have a whole range of needs and interests, objectives and values. This means that religions or cultures as such cannot clash, but only human beings who define their faith or their political objectives and so on in particular ways. But people can come together to take collective action even if their culturally imbued motives differ. They can also blend together impulses from different traditions in new and creative ways; it is quite wrong to believe that each individual can only look at the world from one perspective and that other perspectives must remain inaccessible. In fact, our internal pluralism and the pluralism of the world in which we live correspond to each other.[7] People may also discover new areas of common ground of which they previously had no idea and they may seek to orient themselves by values that cannot be regarded as the exclusive property of one's own community but that relate to all of humanity. The spread of Christianity in the late Roman Empire, for example, appears to have been fostered in significant part by the readiness of Christians to help anyone, not just other Christians.[8] This tells us nothing about the specific dangers of religiously motivated political—or politically motivated religious—conflicts. My sole aim here was to reject the notion of inevitable clashes between different religious traditions.[9]

The second objection takes seriously a factual reality, namely, the wide-scale de-Christianization of East Germany, for example, but also of a fair number of major cities in what used to be West Germany. But this criticism fails to describe this reality with sufficient precision. Intact religious milieus continue to exist alongside largely secularized ones; countless buildings, symbols, rituals, norms, and values continue to speak of a religious past that people may regain an awareness of and that they are quick to recognize, at least as a force that has shaped culture. In addition, the religious vitality of Muslim immigrants represents a challenge to the secularist self-image, while Christian immigrants may help revitalize Christian communities. Low figures on church attendance or church membership do not, moreover, necessarily mean that all those who do not attend or do not belong to a church see themselves as nonreligious. What we need, then, is a self-understanding of religions whose articulation reaches out both to those schooled in a particular faith and to those whose knowledge of it is limited, or who have a good knowledge of it but have turned away. At least in the case of the latter two groups, the same condition applies that I have identified in relation to productive interreligious dialogue. If there is no attempt to relate faith and all value commitments and interpretations of the world to constitutive experiences, we cannot set in motion a genuine and honest debate between believers and nonbelievers. But if we do make this connection clear, then nonbelievers can make their own interpretation of the world more transparent while believers can gain a new awareness of the meaning of the truths of their faith.

My reflections so far have left the issues of a genuine political ethics and the affinities between religions and specific political values (such as democracy) largely untouched. This emphasis on the religious sphere in a narrower sense is based on reservations about attributing an inherent political ethics to religions in the first place.[10] These days, we tend to ascribe a self-evident tendency towards democracy and human rights to Christianity. It is hard to maintain this in light of history. It would be more appropriate to trace the historical trajectory of the development of Christian justifications for democracy and human rights. Through this cautious and self-critical—rather than triumphalist—perspective on the history of Christianity, we could build bridges to the search for religious justifications for democracy and human rights in other religious traditions. In this way, religious traditions could enter into an interreligious dialogue about political ethics without reducing their dialogue to this topic. It would also become clear that it is the ethos of democracy and human rights that has inspired the idea of interreligious dialogue itself. What we are dealing with here is a universalism that does not expect people to break with the particular binding force of the traditions in light of which they understand themselves. To demand such a break, to call for a transition to rational universalisms, for justifications lacking in self-reflexive experiential anchorage and binding force, would in fact be counterproductive.

In engaging with other religions, we have an obligation to adopt this dialogic attitude even if we lack a specific partner in dialogue or if others refuse to engage in such dialogue. In political terms, we can and should combat religiously motivated hostility to democracy and human rights; but our engagement with other religions must be geared not to combat but to productive dialogue. This dialogue links together religious and secular forms of moral and legal universalism. All stand opposed to racist or other forms of anti-universalism, to the postmodern renunciation of universal validity claims, and to attempts to elevate any of the competing universalisms into the only possible one. Through dialogue, universalisms discover their own particularity, previously hidden to them.

8

Religion and Violence

   This chapter begins with a lengthy comment of a personal hue. But I hope it takes us beyond the personal to the heart of the issue I want to get to grips with here. For around two decades, my two main empirical fields have been the sociology of war and violence, on the one hand, and the sociology of religion and values, on the other. Yet during this entire period I have contributed practically nothing to the seemingly obvious task of linking these two fields, despite an avalanche of invitations to speak or write on the connection between religion and violence—particularly after September 11, 2001. My reluctance to embrace this topic was initially purely spontaneous and intuitive. It was probably the result of an aversion to the tacit presuppositions of those asking such questions. Over the past century, the greatest crimes against humanity of all time were carried out by secular-utopian Communist regimes and by the Nazis. Tragically, the latter enjoyed substantial support from numerous Christians, but they actually aimed to overcome and eliminate all transcendence-based religion. In light of such crimes, I did not (and do not) see how anyone can truly believe that the greatest danger to peace lies in religious faith. In this context, faith is often treated thoughtlessly as something dangerously irrational that can be rendered harmless only if it is relegated to the private sphere. Astonishingly, meanwhile, secular reason is just as sweepingly portrayed as peaceful and enlightened.

   Of course, we must also be suspicious of our own spontaneous reluctance. It may be that, enraptured by the beauty of faith, we are simply unwilling to acknowledge the dangers thrown up by religion, that we routinely trivialize the misdeeds carried out in the name of faith, selectively perceiving only those things close to our own values. Even when I examine this closely, it clashes with what I believe about myself. But there is a great deal of this in the external perception of Christianity. Having "learned" from such things as Dan Brown's thrillers or Karlheinz Deschner's criminal history of Christianity,[1] many contemporaries tend, to use Charles Taylor's clever phrase, to regard every Catholic as if he or she is working day and night to revive the Inquisition. Sometimes we must refrain from engaging with a particular question if we wish to avoid perpetuating the questioner's nonsensical presuppositions.

But there is another reason for my resistance—and this is of greater scientific significance. Schooled in American pragmatism, and in the sociology of Max Weber and other German thinkers who made the transition from historicism to modern social science, I am accustomed to analyzing every phenomenon in terms of human action. From this perspective, "religion" and "violence" are only understandable and explicable if we relate them to the experiences and actions with which they are linked. Right at the start, then, we can see that religions are in no sense entities that can act—any more, we might add, than cultures or civilizations, which is why the thesis of their "clash" appears to be a categorical misconception right from the outset. The concept of religion is an abstraction in a dual sense. First, it abstracts from the diversity of faiths, which are so different that generalizing statements about such things as their political significance seem doomed to failure. I am surprised to hear people refer to the indispensability of "religion" to democracy. The speaker presumably does not imply, for instance, that democracy has a special affinity with indigenous Australian totemism. Max Weber, originally trained as a jurist, began almost every chapter of the work that has come down to us as *Economy and Society* with pedantic definitions, but not the chapter on religion, in which he explicitly states that it is impossible to come up with an objective definition in advance; this, he claims, can only be obtained after surveying the diversity of the relevant phenomena.[2]

But there is also another sense in which the notion of "religion" in the singular is an abstraction, one that can be highly misleading if we are unaware of it. We should not conceive even of the most devout individuals as exclusively *religious*. All those with religious convictions find themselves in complex life situations. They have a diverse range of physical and mental needs and economic and political interests that do not simply arise from their religion. No one lives constantly in extraordinary circumstances; how we lead our everyday lives is not completely shaped by the meaningful orientations we have gained through extraordinary experiences. You may believe in a river god while also knowing that dams protect against floods. So we must study the action of religious individuals and communities in specific situations and avoid acting as if we can infer deductively from a given religion what it means for this action.

Much the same applies to the understanding of violence. Again, this is not an entity to which we can meaningfully ascribe specific characteristics. Certainly, much of conventional research on violence is structured in such a way as to imply that what matters most are the perpetrators' specific sociostructural traits, such as social disadvantages, which make it rational to use violence against the better-off or oppressors, or perhaps against scapegoats or in such a way as to raise public awareness through the shocking nature of their acts. But this analysis of violence is just as flawed as attempts to derive the explanation of violent acts from particular values and norms, such as a traditional culture of violence, or from the lack of values, such as a general permissiveness or radical individualism. Both explanatory modes share a common deficiency. They have relatively little to say about the particular point in time when an outbreak of violence begins, the inner dynamics of a violent event or its spread.

We should not misunderstand dissatisfaction with social injustices or negative attitudes towards particular categories of fellow citizens as a kind of preliminary stage in the propensity for violence. For many individuals, dissatisfaction or prejudice give rise to many things, but not to acts of violence, and, conversely, many acts of violence are indiscriminate with respect to victims. So when we talk about violence, we must think about the *interpersonal* dynamics of escalation and the *intrapersonal* dynamics of the consequences of experienced violence for the action of specific individuals.[3]

Right from the start, then, we are going to misconceive the relationship between "religion" and "violence"—and this is what we are thinking about when we ask about religions' compatibility with peace—if we understand it as a relationship between two entities and then go on merely to examine this relationship for causal regularities. If we are to make meaningful statements at all, we must first "ground" both sides of this relationship with respect to people's actions and experiences.

This is all the more important given that the motives that lead people to ask such questions—often expressed in a distorted way—are in fact very understandable and often truly pressing. To get at whether religions are compatible with peace, beyond the shift of perspective I have recommended so far, it is important to clearly distinguish four issues that often interpenetrate when authors tackle these topics. The first concerns the relationship between the sacred and violence. This touches on the most elementary level of religious theory. The second issue relates to *the* epochal shift in the history of religion captured in the term Axial Age. This includes debates on the connection between monotheism and violence. The third issue relates to learning processes in the post-Axial Age religions with respect to their own potential for violence, and thus the religious routes to religious freedom, democracy, and peace. And the fourth issue is concerned with the dynamics of present-day violence-producing conflicts and their religious dimension.

In what follows I outline some attempts to answer these four questions. This lays the basis for my view of the necessary preconditions for religions to promote peace, which I set out in the conclusion in light of a specific conception of the prerequisites for peace.

The sacred and violence

First, we must consider the uncanny structural similarity between ecstatic experiences of self-transcendence and the experience of violence. We belittle the experience of the sacred outrageously if we understand it merely as an effective binding agent for communities or societies. Apart from anything else, this clashes with the profound ambivalence of the experience of the sacred (Rudolf Otto's "tremendum"),[4] in which fascination and terror are indissolubly linked. This is why the sacred is always experienced as dangerous, as something that must be carefully fenced in, or that we should approach only after taking ritual precautions, or after initiation by the more experienced. To the extent that the experience of the sacred represents a stepping beyond everyday life, it temporarily suspends the norms that guarantee peaceful coexistence in everyday life. Because of this, circumstances of collective ecstasy (or "effervescence" as Durkheim put it)[5] often spill over into the dissolution of sexual boundaries and acts of violence. Religions are grounded in such processes of release and in the attempt to control what has been released. Max Weber's famous "Intermediate Reflections" in his comparative studies on the economic ethics of the world religions should not really be read, as they usually are, as evidence of the differentiation of value spheres in modern societies. In fact, they provide a nuanced typology of the competitive relations between different kinds of experience of self-transcendence: religious, aesthetic, and erotic experiences, but also violent ones. So no religion can have a neutral relationship with the other forms of self-transcendence. It must either oppose these other forms of access to the experience of self-transcendence as illegitimate, and thus idealize such things as chastity, nonviolence, or simplicity—or, conversely, it must interpret these experiential paths as forms of the religious and thus, for example, sacralize the erotic (as in tantra or among the hippies), place art in the service of religious experience (as in the ecstatic baroque of Bavarian churches or in Bach's music) or stylize violence as "holy war" in the struggle against enemies of the Faith (as in the Crusades or among the terrorists of September 11, 2001).

There is a fine line between a sober willingness to acknowledge the ambivalence of the sacred as the most elementary layer of religion and mythologizations of this idea. The latter assert that the experience of violence itself produces those much longed-for forces capable of binding together modern societies, which supposedly threaten to disintegrate into an atomized mass of individuals. During World War I, for example, thinkers such as Georg Simmel crossed this line when they interpreted the experience of war as the existential experience of an "absolute situation." This refers to the affective experience of actors who perceive that their devotion and self-sacrifice, up to and including a readiness to die, extend beyond all rational considerations and discursive justifications, and thus experience a value as unconditionally valid. After the war, this motif lived on in the fascist de-moralization of violence under Mussolini and in Carl Schmitt's political existentialism—but also in the reflections, which were antifascist in intent, of the peculiar group of surrealist Durkheimians who called themselves the "Collège de sociologie" (Bataille, Caillois). Roger Caillois especially interpreted aspects of modern war—such as its tremendous waste of material resources, license for violence, which always far exceeds what is immediately necessary in an instrumental sense, and ecstatic fraternization among fellow combatants or entire nations—as a modern form of collective ecstasy in the sense described by Durkheim with respect to tribal religions.[6]

But we can only really prevent ourselves from lapsing into mythologization if we distinguish the social reality of modern wars more carefully from the mere projection upon them of hopes of redemption—and bring out with conceptual clarity the difference between stirring experiences of self-transcendence and traumatizing experiences of violence. In terms of its biographical impact, the involuntary opening of identificatory boundaries resembles those experiences that inspire our values. But it also differs from them. In the case of violence, those affected are unable to put forward any value-affirming narrative, or can only do so if they have more or less recovered from the trauma. Just as value-constitutive experiences of self-transcendence transform one's self-image, the pleasure that may be taken in violent acts also reveals to the perpetrators something about themselves—but in such a way that they may feel a sense of self-betrayal when they experience sides of themselves that, after the experience, no longer seem acceptable.[7]

I have merely given a brief indication of the affinities and parallels between the sacred and violence that must be faced if we wish to study religions' compatibility with peace—and not just that of religions, since what has been said so far inevitably applies to all forms of sacralization, including the sacralization of such things as secular values. The sacralization of the nation or of a supposedly superior race (not just in Nazism but also colonialism and imperialism) was particularly prone to unleash violence against minorities or others classified as "uncivilized" or "parasitical."

The Axial Age and violence

But my remarks so far only relate to the most elementary layer of religions. In the so-called Axial Age, religious history itself generates the strongest reaction to that dynamic of violence inherent in the tribal religions, but particularly in the archaic religions, that is, under conditions of early statehood. René Girard, whose name all those in the know will surely have missed in my remarks so far, offers a highly simplified picture of the basic problems of social life in pre–Axial Age cultures, but hits the nail on the head in seeing the religious overcoming of the scapegoat mechanism in the self-sacrifice of Jesus Christ.[8] Robert Bellah, Charles Taylor, and David Martin see one of the key characteristics of the ethicization of the idea of salvation (Max Weber) in the Axial Age in the radical change in notions of sacrifice. Self-sacrifice rather than the heroic use of violence, universalism rather than blood-brotherhood against enemies, the transcendence of the "source of all holiness" against sacralization of the earthly ruler or earthly political orders—these are the key Axial Age achievements.

Of course, there is a grave risk of misunderstanding these statements when they are made in such sweeping and abbreviated form. But this is not the place for a nuanced account of the various dimensions of the Axial Age breakthrough, the specifics of its further development and potential regressive tendencies.[9] Within a self-reflective religious framework, we clearly have to distinguish between the historical layers of ancient Judaism—as available to us in the "Old Testament," if hard to disentangle—in an attempt to identify its potential for violence, and to discuss the message of the teachings, impact, death, and resurrection of Jesus Christ as a specific development of this tradition. We would also have to explore Islam, with its radical focus on transcendence, the exemplary role of the Prophet Muhammad, and its own version of Axial Age sacrificial mythology (particularly among the Shia), as well as the ethics of Buddhism, which constantly converges with Christianity to a quite astonishing degree, although nourished by a very different religious imagination.

Neither is this the place to take a systematic look at the rights and wrongs of the Assmann thesis,[10] according to which one of the Axial Age variants, namely, Jewish monotheism, was not, as suggested here, a decisive step in religious self-reflection on the potential violence of the sacred, but instead a source of violence. On this view, in the shape of monotheism, a faith centered on the distinction between the one true God and false gods supplanted a naturally tolerant polytheism that could be flexibly supplemented with new gods. In exegetical and religious history terms, this idea has been widely discussed over the past few years. I believe Jan Assmann has de facto retracted it, but it continues to have an impact. It is a remarkable phenomenon for two reasons, which are apparent even before we get down to examining it in detail. In its reception, the claimed potential for violence of the true/false distinction is often related only to monotheism and not to the other Axial Age breakthrough that works with it, which played a major role in the work of Karl Jaspers: namely, the emergence of thinking about thinking in Greek philosophy. But this both loses sight of the potential for violence in a hegemonically inclined secular rationality and carelessly attributes a propensity for violence to the religious conception of truth as such. Further, those espousing this critique fail to see that it is impossible to formulate it consistently if they wish to uphold the liberal conception of tolerance, since this conception cannot be tolerant with respect to its understanding of tolerance. A value-rational understanding of tolerance affirms that all kinds of views have a right to exist, but not opposition to tolerance. The notion that it is only possible to overcome violence by eschewing true/false distinctions becomes consistent, not through Ulrich Beck's "both/and" trope, but through the radical relativization of the entire moral sphere; an example is Carl Schmitt's argument that it is the sense of moral superiority that has led to the worst atrocities. But again, repetition does not make this argument any truer. In empirical terms, it is simply not the case that over the course of history the tendency to unleash violence has been found chiefly among warring factions of a moral-universalist persuasion.[11] In this sense, I agree with those (such as Rolf Schieder) who see the emphasis on transcendence as the decisive Axial Age distinction, "an elementary distinction that warns every true believer not to appoint himself God's mouthpiece or sword. This distinction stands opposed to any pretension that it is possible to act in his name."[12]

The learning history of Christianity

But does this emphasis on transcendence really prevent violence? We have to distinguish between an empirical and normative meaning of the word "prevent." In an empirical sense, the believers of post–Axial Age religions are obviously not immune to conceiving of themselves as God's "mouthpiece" or "sword" and acting accordingly. There is no need for me to run through the entire history of "Christianity between Bible and sword," as Arnold Angenendt has done in his book *Toleranz und Gewalt* (2008; Tolerance and Violence);[13] its chapters teem with examples of violence such as the killing of heretics, persecution of witches, Crusades, confessional wars, persecution of Jews, and colonial crimes. When George W. Bush was battling John Kerry for the American presidency, a remarkable confrontation occurred (in one of the televized debates) over whether people should invoke God in support of American causes or Americans ought to ask themselves whether their actions are justified before God. Kerry's clear enunciation of the distinction between these two different views of the relationship between religion and politics was, of course, a reference to a famous dictum attributed to Abraham Lincoln, but also expressed a tension deeply embedded in all post–Axial Age religions. All of them run the risk of a missionary universalism that may lapse into the ideological cloaking of self-interest.[14] In religious terms, this represents a process of remagification, coercion of the god rather than worship of the god, a regression to pre–Axial Age conditions. But as Wolfgang Huber has asserted with respect to Christianity, all of them are also attempts to develop the strength to "make the potential for violence in human life a subject of discussion rather than denying it, to approach it directly rather than legitimizing it, to acknowledge the human propensity for violence while opposing every attempt to glorify violence, to eschew illusionary efforts to detract attention away from violence, and to challenge violence rather than allowing it to hold sway."[15]

In this sense, rather than being a secure cultural possession, the Axial Age religious achievements are a thorn in the side of civilization with ongoing effects. So the term "prevention" has a normative sense here as well. This means that we must not write a triumphalist history of Christianity as the gradual unfolding of a religious view of humanity, up to and including the liberal-democratic state and the human rights declarations and agreements produced by the international community. We must instead write a contingent history of ever-new reparticularizations of universalism, of the retribalization and nationalization of Axial Age religions, each with their particular potential for violence. Here we must clear away a plethora of historical myths that present the origin of guaranteed religious freedom as lying in Christianity in general or in

European culture since the medieval Investiture Controversy or in the Reformation itself. But the destruction of these myths—as performed in recent times for the Reformation and the outcome of the confessional wars by Wolfgang Reinhard, Horst Dreier, and José Casanova[16]—must not be a means of supporting the secularist myth that sees in religions an inexpungible potential for violence. Instead, it must sensitize us to the historical genesis of the religious motivation to institutionalize religious freedom and individuals' fundamental freedoms in general. It is because of this that I continue to attribute epoch-making significance to Georg Jellinek's 1895 book on the origin of religious freedom in America,[17] which was, of course, the model for Max Weber's studies of Protestantism.[18] Jellinek did *not* assert that Protestantism entails any general tendency to acknowledge each individual's religious freedom. Instead, he sought to show how a very specific processing of the experience of religious persecution by an outsider, the Baptist preacher Roger Williams, in basically theocratic seventeenth-century Massachusetts, could inspire a crucial idea: since each individual's authentic relationship to God depends on his religious freedom, we must inevitably want this freedom for everybody; for every Christian, but also for "Jews, heathens and Turks," and aspire to guarantee this freedom in law as an inalienable, sacrosanct right held by individuals. Among Baptists, Quakers, and other "stepchildren of the Reformation" (Troeltsch) there was a fusion of growing religious individualization and religiously motivated tolerance. I interpret this as the next enormous step forward in religious reflection on the potential for violence inherent in religion. In terms of its logical structure, what this brought into the world—an individual right to freedom guaranteed but not conferred by the state—was something to which many others could relate, including deists (such as Thomas Jefferson) and secularists (such as some of those involved in the French Revolution) but also mainline Protestants, Catholics (through the Second Vatican Council in doctrinal terms, although earlier in many cases), and Muslims. As with every other stage of religious development, there is a risk of regression. But this religious foundation of the modern democratic constitutional state, a state that guarantees peace and freedom domestically, is one of the conditions of its stability; it would be absurd to weaken this in response to secularist attempts at justification. American religious economists have sought, interestingly and I believe persuasively, to demonstrate that religiously charged violent conflicts in societies do not come about through the encounter of different religions as such (as the "clash of civilizations" thesis would lead us to expect) but through the particularist state regulation of religious life, regulation that seeks to aid one particular religious community while keeping another under control.[19] What this means is that nothing contributes more to the peaceful coexistence of a number of religions in a state as the absence of state regulation of the religious "market."

Within German peace research, the nuanced accounts produced by Andreas Hasenclever have plausibly shown that ethnic identities, political ideologies and religious convictions are easy to instrumentalize to particular ends in political conflicts, thus tending to "add fuel to the fire"— although they did not start it in the first place. It is "entrepreneurs of violence," acting in a relatively rational way, who tap into religious traditions for strategic reasons—and generally with greater success when, perhaps after a long period of repression, people have a merely superficial knowledge of their own religion. Crucially important at such moments is whether the "professional" representatives of religious communities (priests, bishops, and theologians in the case of Christianity) argue against this instrumentalization or help advance it. There is nothing inevitable about this; everything is mediated by human action.[20]

Religion and international conflicts

So far, I have been careful to refer only to peace within societies, since we cannot simply extrapolate the preconditions for peaceful conduct towards the rest of the world from the preconditions for its establishment domestically. This would be possible only if the thesis, which was fashionable for a while, that democracies as such are more peaceful than other states, were tenable, but this is simply not the case.[21] Because of this, in principle, we must go one step further and ask what role religions play in international conflicts or military clashes between states and nonstate antagonists. Again, I can only provide an answer in outline here. But it is vital to provide such an answer if we wish to establish religions' capacity for peace in view of global challenges. We would otherwise merely perpetuate the social sciences' venerable tendency to limit themselves to processes within societies and ignore the constitutive importance of exogenous factors and international constellations.

Over the past two decades, public debates on violent conflicts under the conditions of globalization have been dominated by two buzzwords: "clash of civilizations" and "new wars." I have already explained my fundamental skepticism about the first thesis at the beginning of this chapter when I tackled the false stylization of cultures (or religions) as subjects capable of action. There are strong empirical grounds for rejecting the thesis of the clash of civilizations.[22] But the notion of wars of a "new" type—that is, unconventional, "post-Clausewitzean" wars, often verging on terrorism and crime—also loses much of its plausibility if we rise above a Eurocentric perspective. Even in the heyday of nation-states, wars between states were actually the exception. This is immediately evident if we include conflicts in and over colonies. "Much of the killing in this period [i.e., the mid-nineteenth century] arose from low-intensity conflicts that were ongoing, undecided, periodically genocidal, had recurring edges of terrorism and may be thought of as local wars."[23] Furthermore, in the writings of those expounding the "new wars" theory, it is very unclear how claims of the growing significance of de-ideologized markets in violence relate to—often accompanying—references to the supposed religious causes of conflict.

More fruitful from a religion-focused perspective is Hans Gerhard Kippenberg's attempt,[24] heavily influenced by the work of Max Weber, to present a nuanced discussion of the interplay of religious and political-economic realities by looking at one of the key trouble spots of our time: Israel/Palestine. This attempt is characterized by the methodological desideratum I identified in the introduction: Kippenberg does not treat religions as actors isolated from the rest of social life. Instead, he shows how, through an insidious process, a conflict that was by no means originally religious in nature has increasingly been defined in religious terms by three different camps. The Zionists were initially overwhelmingly secular; the Palestinians long sought their salvation in Arab nationalism and to some extent in Marxism; American foreign policy under Presidents Truman and George W. Bush stood in a complex relationship to the worldview of certain Protestant fundamentalists who imbued the conflict with eschatological significance. While a religious interpretation of the conflict by those involved may certainly exacerbate the conflict or hamper its resolution, Kippenberg rejects the notion that a religious interpretation must inevitably involve such options. Instead, he identifies a conflict-exacerbating effect in cases in which, "with regard to faith communities that come into conflict with government authorities or with the legal systems, a vocabulary is employed that speaks of 'cults,' 'fundamentalism' or 'terror groups,' thus denying them any genuinely religious character and excluding them as negotiating partners."[25] From this perspective, it is not Islam, the Jewish religion in Israel, or the specific Protestantism that exists in the United States *as such* that triggers conflict or renders it insoluble. It is, in fact, the political instrumentalization of religions on all sides, and the distorted construction of other religions among the different parties to conflict, that hinder resolution of the conflict. In concrete terms, Kippenberg would like to see a less hostile attitude towards Hamas; he places his hopes in transreligious civil society initiatives and supranational institutions of conflict resolution.

This brings us to the end of my run through the four thematic complexes into which we must, I believe, subdivide the question of the connection between religion and violence. The key topics were the relationship between the sacred and violence and between the Axial Age and violence; the history of Christianity with respect to the religious roots of religious freedom and modern freedom generally; and the religious dimension of international conflicts in our time. I would like to close by setting out three theses that elucidate my answer to the question of religions' capacity for peace.

1. Religions help promote peace if they have incorporated the rejection of primeval notions connecting sacredness and violence, have overcome the risk of the particularist reduction of Axial Age universalism through state exploitation of religion, and have generated religious motives for the institutionalization of individual liberties.

2. Religions help promote peace if they resist attempts to instrumentalize them politically and the construction of religious and other notions of the Enemy and thus help engender the cultural prerequisites for international peace.

3. Such peace-promoting religions are not simply "modern" religions; they reject the identification of a specific institutional order with modernity as such, and continue to act as an Axial, transcendence-focused but practical, worldly thorn in the flesh of political and social life, one that constantly drives it forward.

9

The Future of Christianity

For a social scientist, talking about the future is a risky business. The joke that predictions are particularly difficult when they relate to the future is far from new. The establishment of a new scientific discipline called "futurology" was a very short-lived fashion during a period of unbridled faith in science.

Indeed, it is quite true that the social sciences in no way predicted a series of spectacular developments over the past few decades. Key examples are widely known. They extend from the international student rebellions of the late 1960s, which broke out at the very point when scholars were publishing studies on university students' resistance to political participation, through the rapid economic rise of East Asia, to the collapse of communist rule in Eastern Europe and the Soviet Union.[1] All these developments surprised scholarly experts, but the same goes for journalists and even the secret services—reason enough, then, to eschew any tendency for mutual disparagement, but also for humility on all sides. This admonition applies even more when it comes to predictions about religious developments. The history of religions is particularly rich in new departures, revivals and ruptures that make a mockery of any notion of linear historical processes. The growing politicization of Shia Islam in Iran was widely noticed only with the fall of the Shah, while the sensational expansion of Pentecostalism in Africa and Latin America over the past few decades has yet to truly penetrate the consciousness of the Western public. Believers should not really be surprised by such fundamental surprises, since they expect to see the workings of God in history and maintain hope against all the odds. But even the secular-minded will concede that optimism and abundant self-belief are basic preconditions for individual and collective creativity, and that belief in a future sometimes helps generate this mentality. This is what we call a self-fulfilling prophecy.

Until a few years ago, one prediction about the future of religion went virtually unchallenged among academics and the general public. This was that modernization would inevitably entail irreversible and radical secularization. For the most part, all that remained unclear was what exactly the term "secularization" means—declining church membership, a falloff in participation in religious rituals, or a weakening of individual faith itself? Or merely the withdrawal of faith into the private sphere, whatever this might be taken to mean? In recent times, however, for many good reasons, this prediction has lost much of its plausibility[2]—to such an extent that many commentators have now reversed course and refer to the "return" of religion or "the gods" or claim we are now living in a "post-secular society." All of these ideas, it seems to me, are based on the false assumption that religion had disappeared in the past while exaggerating the extent of the change that has now occurred. Even those who wish to see faith strengthened should keep a level head here. At the moment all that has changed is the focus of attention, above all in the media, along with the balance of forces in intellectual life. The weakening of the notion of an automatically advancing process of secularization certainly opens up opportunities to faith, but these have yet to be exploited. And as far as diagnosis and prognosis are concerned, the thesis of secularization has yet to be replaced with plausible scenarios of a religious future. I can sum up my empirical-sociological remarks on this topic, which, of course, only concern certain aspects of it, in three key phrases: the dissolution of milieus, implicit religion, and the globalization of Christianity.

The dissolution of milieus and the development of a transconfessional Christian milieu

Many accounts have described the situation of Christians in Germany by contrasting the closed political and lifeworldly milieus of the past with the alleged profound individualization of the present. There is undoubtedly a lot of truth in this conventional view, but I would like to correct certain aspects of it. An important study on "religious socialization, confessional milieus and generations," for example, has produced two remarkable findings with reference to the city of Cologne.[3] The dissolution of confessional milieus has indeed made it more difficult for families to pass on their faith. The factual decline in this transmission appears to confirm the expectation that families often fail in this endeavor as a result. But if we take account of differing degrees of the intensity of religious practice, a different picture emerges. In certain cases, the success of religious transmission has actually increased. So while the group of the strongly religious has become smaller, it has become more successful in passing on religious tradition. But the role of confessions has diminished. Data on marriage behavior confirm that the dividing line runs ever less between the confessions and their milieus and increasingly between Christians and non-Christians. There is considerable indication that although the Christian milieu in Germany has become smaller, it is vibrant, and its transconfessional character is beginning to emerge. In order to appreciate this, we must, of course, bear in mind that present-day milieus are less characterized by spatial concentration than they used to be, because telephones and improved transportation have made it easier to maintain contact and coordinate activities despite considerable distances.[4]

We should resist any temptation to retrospectively idealize the vanishing "Catholic" milieu. After all, it came into existence in Germany defensively rather than in an entirely voluntary manner, in opposition to modernization, Protestantism, nationalism, liberalism, and a secularist labor movement. Drawing on analyses of the Netherlands, commentators saw this as an aspect of the "pillarization" of German society, the tendency for milieus to seal themselves off from one another. As long as it existed, this pillarization was rightly regarded as an obstacle to the development of a national democratic political culture in Germany; so many responded with a sigh of relief when the gap between the milieus began to close and the pillars began to crumble in the 1960s.[5] The Catholic milieu in particular was often intellectually and culturally stagnant. In Germany, moreover, it had lived through the Nazi era and had by no means proven immune to it. Political authoritarianism and xenophobic cultural homogeneity were inherent in a milieu that Karl Rahner described as "local-outfit

Catholicism" (*Trachtenvereinskatholizismus*), which evokes a Catholicism akin to Germany's societies promoting traditional dress—and I believe this hits the nail on the head.

Many unpleasant things could also be said about the various political expressions of German Protestantism, such as its submissive attitude to the state, which became increasingly tinged with nationalism following the foundation of the Bismarck Empire, and the anti-Catholicism of many former Protestants who have long since bid farewell to their Protestant faith. So the question for the future of Christianity cannot simply be how milieus can be stabilized or saved, as if social disintegration was the necessary consequence of a change of milieu. Instead, the question must be how values can be passed on in new ways amid such a change of milieu and how they can arise anew through new experiences. It may be that values and faith are sometimes poorly transmitted precisely because they are in a sense shut up in a milieu. There has been a tendency for some in the Catholic milieu to lose sight of the message of the Gospel.

It is noteworthy that there are comparable developments in the United States, which is characterized, not by the kind of state-protected biconfessionalism found in Germany, but by religious pluralism and the strong separation of state and churches. It has long been noted that individuals are paying less and less attention to theological differences, particularly between the different forms of Protestantism, while individuals' political and moral affinities with particular religious communities are proving decisive to their appeal.[6] This, of course, also has consequences for the selection of friends and spouses. Recent research, carried out on a broad empirical basis,[7] has shown a great increase in the number of interconfessional marriages over the past few decades. Today, the majority of new marriages are "interfaith." The notion of traditional religious communities sealed off from one another, which was still plausible in the 1950s, is increasingly losing any connection with reality. The religious landscape of the United States is constantly changing as a result of the emergence of new Christian churches that cannot be assigned to any major historical denomination. The fact that religious communities and social milieus do not coincide is another reason why religious intensity and religious tolerance are often interlinked.

Implicit religion

My second key term, "implicit religion," refers to the multifarious values and practices that constitute an "ultimate point of reference" and are "super-relevant" (Detlef Pollack) for those concerned. The term thus refers to everything that we might call religion, but that its practitioners do not describe as such, and to those activities that participants refer to as religion, but that are not really accepted as such by others. With the decline of church-related religiosity, researchers became increasingly interested, Pollack notes, in "non-church forms of religious orientation, new religious movements, new-age psychocults, occultism, spiritualism or cultic milieus . . . , the Neo-Sannyas [Rajneesh] movement, neo-Germanic paganism, Bach flower remedies, Qigong, Zen meditation and the 'small world' of bodybuilders, the unfamiliar world of dowsers and pendulum diviners, the self-image and worldviews of 'postmodern' youth, and even the cult of football or popular music,"[8] or in political movements and "political religions," as Eric Voegelin called the totalitarian movements of the twentieth century.[9] In analytical terms, it is not helpful to extend the concept of religion so far that it excludes the possibility of secularization by definition. This does not seem compatible to me with the reality of places such as eastern Germany, one of the most secularized regions in the world. And I believe Pollack is correct to reject the idea that the decline in church-related religiosity and "the gains of new religious movements, esoteric groups and East Asian spirituality" relate to one another like a system of communicating tubes, in which "there can be no loss of substance but at most a process of redistribution." Quantitatively speaking, the situation is in fact unambiguous: church losses are not being balanced out by gains in other areas—in Europe. In the United States, on the other hand, the shift towards individualistic spirituality tends to occur within religious communities rather than outside of or in opposition to them. None of this, however, justifies ignorance about the forms and tendencies of footloose religiosity or so-called casual piety.

The globalization of Christianity

My third key term is "the globalization of Christianity." If we are to analyze religion in the present day, it is vital to adopt a global, that is, non-Eurocentric perspective. The very idea that the nineteenth century was an era of secularization is (partially) valid only in the case of Europe. In the United States, church membership grew continuously in both absolute and relative terms during this period, and in the rest of the world a variety of developments occurred with regard to religion, with one notable exception: secularization. In Africa, Christianity and Islam became broadly disseminated through missionary activities; in Asia and the Islamic world, religious traditions responded to the challenge of Christianity and European power in a great variety of ways. Even those contemporary social scientists who continue to adhere to the notion of the secularizing effects of modernization—such as Ronald Inglehart, prominent researcher on value change—now make different kinds of predictions about the religious situation of the world, taking greater account of the demographic aspect of developments.[10] If, they argue, secularization has a negative impact on birthrates, while under present-day conditions, religious orientations, or at least traditional ones, lead to rapid population increase, then religious individuals as a share of the global population will increase dramatically in any case, despite all the assumed secularization. And, of course, this applies even more if, contra Inglehart, we consider the thesis of secularization itself to be wrong and believe that it underestimates the religious vitality of the developed world. Astonishingly, some relate the demographic factor almost exclusively to global Islam, but not global Christianity. Yet many of the most rapidly growing nations are entirely or heavily Christian in character. We need only think of Brazil, Uganda, or the Philippines, whose populations have almost doubled since 1975. The population of some of these countries will again at least double by 2050, radically changing global population rankings. But demography is not the only cause of Christianity's rapid global spread. Against the expectations of critics of colonialism, who believed Christianity had no future as a Western implant in a foreign environment, it was *after* colonial rule came to an end that Christianity began to spread most rapidly in Africa, partly through mass conversions. Estimates suggest that at present the number of Christians in Africa increases by around 23,000 people a day—through birth, but in more than a sixth of cases through conversion. From 1965 to 2001, Christians as a proportion of the African population increased from 25 to 46 percent. Certainly, religious statistics are not terribly reliable; but the trends at least seem indisputable. In Asia, too, Christianity has enjoyed some astonishing successes, most spectacularly in South Korea, where a third of the population now professes the Christian faith. In order to understand the reasons for this, we must look back to the period before the rapid economic modernization of the most recent decades. Highlighting modernization is certainly a powerful way to undermine the thesis of secularization, but does not help us explain the expansion of Christianity.[11] In Korea, the experience of Japanese imperialism and colonization had played an important role, showing that the rejection of a Christianity perceived as Western may give way to a desire for thoroughgoing Westernization. In any case, circumstances favor the linkage of Korean patriotism and Christianity (particularly of the Protestant variety). While there was still severe persecution of Christians in Korea in the nineteenth century, this changed as a result of minorities' role in the struggle against the Japanese and the role of the United States following liberation.[12] I am unwilling to speculate about the religious future of China, but at least in parts of China and among overseas Chinese, Christianity has demonstrated considerable appeal. In the first few decades of Communist rule, China experienced the greatest religious persecution in human history.[13] This led to tremendous destruction and to the large-scale abandonment of religious traditions, particularly during the so-called Cultural Revolution. Even when this was over, the Communist leadership continued to uphold the notion that those religious communities that had not yet disappeared would do so in the foreseeable future. Instead, China today is the largest Buddhist nation in the world, the number of Daoist holy sites has trebled in the past fifteen years, and it appears that in absolute terms more Christians now regularly attend a Christian Sunday service in China than in all of Western Europe. In Latin America, the triumphant advance of Pentecostalism and Protestant sects is clearly more than a short-lived phenomenon.[14] These play a major role for women in particular, who hope they may herald a "reformation of machismo."[15] From a global perspective, then, there is absolutely no reason to take a despairing view of Christianity's prospects of survival. In fact, it appears that we are witnessing one of the most intensive periods of the dissemination of Christianity in its entire history.[16]

These developments will affect Christians in Europe in a wide variety of ways. As far as the Catholic Church is concerned, we are probably on the threshold of a fundamental power shift. Such a shift has, of course, already occurred in the Anglican church. Here there are massive tensions over the understanding and practice of the faith between different parts of the world, novel alliances across great distances, and tendencies to schism. It is extremely difficult to infer anything about the future in light of trends over the past few decades. If the historical experience of Europe and North America is any guide, the growth of Pentecostalism is likely to slow; but the major churches are likely to become more charismatic in competition with it. The relationship between a burgeoning Christianity and Islam, which is also growing across the world, may take on a wide variety of different forms, depending on global political constellations. Migration will make the religious intensity of the "Third World" ever more present in the "First World" as well. Migration today, moreover, no longer means complete detachment from one's home country, so we can probably assume that this will be a two-way flow.

While in the United States immigrants' religious commitments are generally understood in light of their integrative potential, in Europe, the tendency has been to see them as an obstacle to integration. It is one of the effects of such an attitude that in Europe, immigrants are more likely to cope with experiences of rejection and exclusion by making their religious commitments central to an oppositional identity.[17]

The false equation of Christianity with Europe

All of this will loosen the equation of Christianity with Europe or the West. Historically speaking, this was, of course, always problematic. Europe was never as homogeneously Christian as a certain romantic perspective would have had us believe, and in its first few centuries, Christianity was not based predominantly in Europe. The late Ghanian theologian Kwame Bediako was quite right to describe the contemporary globalization of Christianity as the "renewal of a non-Western religion."[18] An anecdote may help elucidate how far many people still are from properly understanding this. While working on his book on Pope Benedict XVI, a well-known German journalist interviewed me. He asked me whether the pope was the new opinion leader of the Western world. When I answered that the pope is not and should not be a spokesperson for the West, he promptly misunderstood my response, assuming that I was denying the pope's importance to the West. But the pope is the most important representative of Christianity, and not of the West, and the next few years will leave no one in any doubt that Christianity is very much more than the West. All three tendencies—dissolution of milieus, footloose religiosity, and the globalization of Christianity—are challenges to the transmission of faith and the intellectual self-understanding of faith in our day. If the nexus of faith and homogeneous social milieus is loosening, if faith finds itself in competition with a whole range of partly secular, partly vaguely religious worldviews and ways of life, if faith is being appropriated afresh in the world beyond those cultural areas long shaped by Christianity and under conditions of mass poverty and displacement—in all these cases, Christianity must be liberated from unnoticed particularisms and articulated anew. This entails significant intellectual challenges.

The future of religious communities in Europe

Each aspect of this outline of religious trends has consequences for the future role of religious communities in Europe.

1. Ecumenical dialogue and cooperation are even more important if I am correct in hypothesizing that we are currently witnessing the development of a transconfessional Christian milieu in Germany—in other words, that there is more to the shift in religious milieus than just the atrophying of confessional milieus. Attempts to mark off the boundaries between the Christian churches are thus losing their underpinnings in corresponding separate milieus; it seems likely that believers will be increasingly disinclined to support such efforts. On a number of occasions the journalist Daniel Deckers has fittingly referred to a reversal in the burden of proof with respect to ecumenical cooperation: it is its absence rather than presence that requires justification.

2. From a Christian perspective, "implicit religion" may seem like an incredible simplification, the relinquishment of a treasure house of wisdom and interaction with the divine accumulated over millennia, a loss of transcendence, or even a form of narcissistic egocentrism. But we may also perceive implicit religion as

entailing multiple sites of interface for the churches that represent both opportunities and spiritual challenges. The Swiss sociologist Franz-Xaver Kaufmann has introduced the term "interaction" (*Wechselwirkung*) to bring out the necessity of such interfacing, but also the opportunities inherent in it: "Only if we succeed in creating an interplay between the churches, which are entrusted with preserving and developing the explicitly Christian dimension, and the forms of implicit Christian practice and communication found in interstitial spaces, can we hope to pass on Christianity to new generations under present-day social conditions."[19] Of course, such attempts and proposals to build bridges between these realms must not cause anybody to squander or undervalue their own traditions. There will certainly be a need to uphold transcendence in the face of trends towards detranscendentalization in both implicit and explicit contemporary religions. But whenever one finds points of contact with experiences and interpretations in this way, one is productively challenged to rearticulate one's own tradition. If it is true that competition intensifies religious life, then both believers and religious institutions must rise to the occasion and meet this competitive challenge.

3. The globalization of Christianity and a religious diversity in Europe that is being reinforced by migration enhance the significance of interreligious dialogue and the cooperation of Christian churches with non-Christian religious communities. Equally, though, there will be a need to find new modes of dialogue between believers and nonbelievers in a constellation that is different from the traditional conflicts in the sphere of religion and politics.[20]

10

Intellectual Challenges for
Contemporary Christianity

The challenges with which Christianity now finds itself confronted are of many different kinds. To gain an overview, it is useful to begin by dividing them into two types: challenges arising from social change and challenges resulting from cultural changes. The preceding chapter dealt with the first type.

In this chapter I take a rather different tack. My concern here is with the intellectual challenges arising from Western culture itself. An article by Ernst Troeltsch published more than a hundred years ago will serve as my conceptual foil here. This gives me the opportunity to identify changes in the past century, to tease out persistent and novel challenges. In 1910, in the journal *Logos*, which he had just founded in collaboration with other intellectual giants such as Max Weber, Edmund Husserl, and Georg Simmel, Ernst Troeltsch published an essay on "The Possible Futures of Christianity." It asked whether Europe faced the imminent emergence of new, as yet unknown religious phenomena, a religion-free future, or the "nascent dissolution of European culture itself, which will prove incapable of forming a new religious element of life, while at the same time being unable to do without this element."[1] Against all such scenarios, pessimistic ones from a Christian standpoint, Troeltsch insisted at least on the possibility that the religious forces of the present might come together in new ways, and that the organization of Christians might undergo profound reform. What he envisaged was the unification of the basic sociological forms of Christianity (church, sects, mysticism) through

the mutual interpenetration of these organizational types, and the reconciliation of the motives underlying them, as he would set out in 1912, in
one of his major works.[2] He saw Christianity's main intellectual challenge
as the increasing lack of understanding of four essential elements of the
Christian message: (1) the ethos of love, (2) the understanding of the person, (3) the communality of worship, and (4) the focus of all spirituality
on Jesus Christ. The challenge, then, is generated—in my language rather
than Troeltsch's—by (1) an intellectual hegemony of values and cognitive
assumptions that make the ethos of love increasingly difficult to understand; (2) a concept of the human being that disputes the special features
of human personhood; (3) an increasingly individualistic understanding
of spirituality, and (4). the loss of the idea of transcendence, without which
people are unable to gain an understanding of the Son of God as the
mediator of immanence and transcendence. I shall now examine all four
points more closely, paying special attention to the intellectual situation
of the present.

The ethos of love

Over the past half-century, two forms of individualism have enjoyed
hegemonic status throughout the Western world. The first of these is
known as "utilitarian" individualism, that is, a "utility-oriented" attitude
to life focused on the gaining of short-term and generally material advantage and the clever selection of action strategies to achieve such goals. The
other hegemonic form of individualism is known as the "expressive" form,
an orientation towards the self-expression or self-realization of the individual and the satisfaction of his or her emotional needs. If we follow the
great American sociologist of religion Robert Bellah and his colleagues,
who helped bring these terms to prominence through their influential 1985
book *Habits of the Heart*,[3] then in simplistic terms, two present-day social
types, which are culturally dominant today in the United States and elsewhere, correspond to these two forms of individualism: the manager to
utilitarian and the therapist to expressive individualism.

There may be great tensions between these two forms of individualism—as seen in the rebellion of an expressivist youth counterculture against
the world of their utility-oriented fathers, the "organization men," in the

1960s and 1970s. But rather than making an existential choice between these two worlds, people may also try to create a harmonious relationship between them. This applies, it seems to me, to so-called yuppie culture, in which people give the pursuit of utility free rein in their professional lives, while at the same time placing great emphasis on aesthetic self-realization in their free time.[4] This leads to the most varied forms of conspicuous consumption (culinary skills, expert knowledge of wines) and the production and marketing of art. The balance between the two forms of individualism is always unstable, and this balance takes very different forms in different countries. It seems obvious to me that over the past few decades the intellectual hegemony of utilitarian individualism, such as the reputation of the microeconomic paradigm of "rational action," was greater in the United States and to some extent the United Kingdom than in continental Europe. This seemed to change as a result of the great financial crisis of 2007–8, which did severe damage to the prestige of bankers and to the discipline of economics, which had not predicted the crisis; it also gave "greed"—which had only recently been justified as socially useful—a bad name as a motive for action. But widespread hopes in certain countries that the crisis was already over, and that they had ultimately got off lightly, rapidly revived the self-confidence of the utilitarian individualists.

It is particularly important that these two forms of egocentric individualism be distinguished from other value traditions that we might also refer to as "individualist," but that are oriented to the value of all individuals, rather than being egocentric or narcissistic. In the American case, Bellah and his co-authors identified two such traditions: the republican and the biblical traditions. The term "republican" here has nothing to do with the political party of this name, but refers to a political tradition that goes back to democracy of the Athenian polis, the Roman Republic, and the late medieval Italian city states. In this tradition, citizens play an active role in political life and have a genuine say in the organization of their polity. These citizens are expected to act virtuously, which simply means that the common good must be more important to them than their individual utility or individual self-realization. As impressive as this tradition is, it was clearly always at risk of pitting the common good of one particular republic against that of other polities. Because of this, the other tradition is even more important from an ethical standpoint. The above authors call this the "biblical" tradition, because they explicitly wish to include the Jewish tradition as well as the Christian one. Moral decentering is fundamental to this tradition: when making decisions people are morally obliged to consider, not only those of their fellows who belong to the same family, republic, nation, religion, or class, but everyone, every human being, including future generations. Such a universalist orientation has been elaborated by philosophers such as Kant, John Rawls, and Jürgen Habermas in detailed reflections on the logic of universalist moral reflection and discussion. Yet it remains unresolved in these impressive intellectual edifices why people should, in fact, be motivated to enter into such processes of reflection when it comes to leading their own lives in a moral way. It is also unclear how sensitization to the suffering of others, which is not after all the result of rational argument, is achieved.[5]

But this is the essence of the superiority of the Christian ethos of love, even over all forms of universalist moral philosophy, and particularly over what I have described here as egocentric forms of individualism. In line with this, the intellectual challenge for Christianity today is to reveal the limits of utilitarian and expressive individualism, elaborate the nonuniversalist character of republican thought, and criticize forms of moral universalism limited by rationalism. This makes it an urgent task to clarify the relationship between "justice" as the key concept of moral and legal universalism and "love" as the key to the Christian ethos. The Christian belief in a God who loves human beings unconditionally certainly has the potential to liberate our own capacity to love unconditionally. As such, however, it does not provide us with complete instructions on how to strike a balance between "love" and "justice" as two dimensions of tremendous importance to any political ethics. Christians are not simply representatives of—in Max Weber's terminology—an "acosmistic" ethos of love. They also believe in justice, but go beyond this belief by refusing to close their minds to the need to repeatedly relativize the principles of justice, so indispensable to the social and political order, through the ethos of love.

Personhood

For many people today, the most profound intellectual challenge to Christianity has a different source, namely, a reinvigorated reductionist "naturalism." We find ourselves confronted with brain researchers who go so far as to dispute the meaning of the term "free will," geneticists who believe their analyses allow us to explain the full range of human behavior or will do so in future, and sociobiologists who understand human action as the mere expression of tendencies inherent in selfish genes. All these commentators attract an astonishing degree of attention, not so much among scholars, as among those who Richard Rorty refers to as "science watchers"—people, in other words, who are interested in science primarily because they imagine it will help them foster a nonreligious worldview.

I call this widespread interest "surprising," because I believe most of the arguments being put forward today with an air of unprecedented natural scientific progress were already being made during the second half of the nineteenth century, and in some cases even earlier. Back then they prompted detailed refutation by, for example, pragmatists and phenomenologists, who took up this challenge by clarifying what distinguishes human action from the behavior of animals and what we actually mean when we talk of free will, and who elaborated the true nature of the symbolic mediation of human drives, the perception of the world, and movement control.[6] It would be fair to say that these arguments and counterarguments have flown back and forth so often that it has become difficult to call this a genuine intellectual challenge.

But this remark by no means implies that it is unimportant to examine the new forms taken by reductionist naturalism and to respond to them by rearticulating Christian personalism. What is less obvious, so it seems to me, is that the defense of the understanding of personhood so vital to Christianity must be carried on, not just on this front, but simultaneously on another front as well. What I have in mind is the historical analysis of what I call the "sacralization of the person." Christians may be convinced that the biblical tradition and especially the Gospels are deeply saturated by an understanding of the sacred core of every human being and express this through ideas such as the immortal soul and human beings as made in the image of God or as the children of God. But this does not mean that they can claim that throughout the history of Christianity, these notions have always guided Christian views of the correct way to organize a political community. On the contrary, it took a very long time even in nominally Christian states for this notion of the dignity of every human being to inspire a commitment to democracy and human rights; the Christian churches have by no means always set the pace here. My own view is that it was only in the eighteenth century, with its human rights declarations in North America and France, that a breakthrough occurred in developments in this respect that are still ongoing today and that by no means hold sway throughout the world. Here, then, the intellectual challenge for Christianity consists first and foremost in the illusion-free and self-critical examination of the connections between Christianity and the "sacralization of the person." What role was and is played by Christians and Christian churches or religious communities in the history of human rights, the abolition of torture, the abolition of slavery, and the overcoming of discrimination against women or sexual minorities? Did they, and do they continue to, justify the perpetuation of realities that are unjustifiable from the perspective of universal human dignity? Part of the challenge here is to avoid misinterpreting insights into the historical change of deep-seated values relativistically, as if the historical genesis of values demonstrates that they cannot lay claim to transtemporal validity and that, in the spirit of Nietzsche and Foucault, we ought to liberate ourselves from their claims.[7]

Spirituality

Today, many people candidly admit that they have "spiritual" needs and experiences—in connection for example with art or eros or in the confrontation with existential crises such as serious illness, the fear of death, or the loss of loved ones. Their spiritual search often prompts an interest in exotic religious traditions, and many seek to engage in spiritual practices. For such people, however, this certainly does not mean that they feel compelled to join a church, because they assume that spirituality is something that can be developed in a purely individual way. They tend to view the church more as an obstacle to the development of their personhood.

Conversely, probably all Christians with ties to a church—and above all Catholics—face incomprehension from their contemporaries when they express concerns, doubts, and anger about the church without questioning their membership of and affiliation to it. This incomprehension is the result of an understanding that is generally unquestioned and taken for granted these days, namely, that social organization must always and everywhere be the product of the voluntary association of its members, and that we should therefore reject the idea of an organization prior and superordinate to this voluntary principle. The idea that the church has this status, that it enables individuals to believe and become themselves in the first place, runs deeply counter to the individualistic tendencies of our time.

Ernst Troeltsch had a polemical way of referring to this individualistic inability to understand the church as a community enabling individuality. He spoke here of the reduction of the church to a "society for worship" (*Kultverein*), a mere setting for the communal practice of rituals that is devoid of any transpersonal character. This is a particularly complicated issue since the understanding of the correct social organization for Christians within Christianity is far from uniform. Catholics and to a certain extent Anglicans, Orthodox Christians, and Lutherans have a strong concept of church, while more radical versions of Protestantism have always taken umbrage at this and considered congregationalist and other purely voluntary forms more appropriate. So we cannot simply refer to an intellectual challenge for Christianity as a whole when it comes to the understanding of the church. Within the Catholic Church alone, a whole range of attempts have been made to achieve an understanding of the church that avoids degrading it to the status of a "society for worship." These extend from authoritarian-hierarchical and excessively centralist solutions of the kind developed by the Catholic Church primarily in the nineteenth century, to the notion of the church as a "network of agape." Guided by the fourfold definition (*una sancta catholica et apostolica*) in the Nicene Creed, Cardinal Karl Lehmann has developed a compelling understanding of the church that is one, but not uniform; holy, but also sinful, and thus always in need of reform; missionary, in the style of the Apostles, from whom it takes its lead; and Catholic in the sense of a concrete universalism that overcomes all that is national and culturally particularist.[8] In this view of confessional distinctions, that which all Christians share must always come first. On the basis of the writings of the great French theologians Henri de Lubac and Yves Congar, Charles Taylor coined the term "network of agape" in his book *A Secular Age*. This is an attempt to assert a specific modernity of the idea of the "church"—and not, of course, its actual reality, which often deviates from this idea: "The life-blood of this new relation is agape, which can't ever be understood simply in terms of a set of rules, but rather as the extension of a certain kind of relation, spreading outward in a network. The church is in this sense a quintessentially network society, even though of an utterly unparalleled kind, in that the relations are not mediated by any of the historical forms of relatedness: kinship, fealty to a chief, or whatever. It transcends all these, but not into a categorical society based on similarity of members, like citizenship; but rather into a network of ever different relations of agape."[9]

For Troeltsch at least, "in this case as much as any other, the autonomy of personal and conscience-based conviction cannot mean a radical absence of tradition or a spontaneity entirely of the moment." What is to be aimed at is "a vibrant process of personal appropriation and further development," the "working through and internalization of historical forces,"[10] not substitution of idiosyncratic worldviews and practices for the historic treasure house of institutional experience.

Transcendence

At the start I reformulated Troeltsch's idea that the spiritual focus on Jesus Christ has become more difficult to understand as the diminishing comprehension of transcendence. This may sound rather mysterious at first. I do not mean the watered-down version of "transcendence," so common in contemporary religious debates, that includes every step outside the quotidian realm. What I mean is the ambitious conception of transcendence developed—although not exclusively—in the Judaism of the so-called Axial Age. This refers to the radical desacralization of all structures of political domination and social inequality as propagated by the prophets. Central components of the Christian faith (the Incarnation, the doctrine of the Trinity) presuppose this "prophetic" conception of transcendence. Without it we cannot grasp the full force of the specifically Christian mediation of transcendence and immanence. This point has emerged as an important intellectual challenge in the interreligious dialogue between the "Abrahamic" religions. But just as important is to go on the offensive against the conscious efforts in the philosophy, culture, and politics of the twentieth century to regress from this demand for a transcendence that relativizes every aspect of earthly existence. I see thinkers such as Martin Heidegger and Georges Bataille and many of their postmodern acolytes as exponents of such "detranscendentalization," along with, though, of course, in different ways, the "political religions" of the past century, such as the Nazi attempts to revive the pre-Christian Germanic religion or the Stalinist self-sacralization of the postrevolutionary order and its political leader. For all those whom we might refer to as post-totalitarian Christians, in other words, for Christians who have gone through the experience of totalitarian repression, but have also experienced, or whose parents have experienced, the totalitarian temptation at first hand, the confrontation with hostility to and loss of transcendence is one of the most important intellectual challenges of the present era.[11]

It is of crucial importance to this task to analyze historically both the emergence of the idea of transcendence and the reasons for its disappearance. This idea emerged in the period between 800 and 200 BC; Karl Jaspers famously coined the term "Axial Age" for an idea that had been around for some time, including in the work of Max Weber.[12] Over the past few decades, the political-moral potential of the idea of transcendence, namely, its capacity to prompt us to question the earthly order, has been elaborated even more clearly than in the work of Weber and Jaspers in concrete historical-sociological terms. What has emerged here is that all the religions that arose during the Axial Age share certain similarities in this respect; there is common ground, for example, between the Abrahamic religions, on the one hand, and Buddhism and Confucianism, on the other. Against all talk of the inevitable clash of civilizations, here is a chance to rediscover what all post-Axial Age religions have in common,[13] and to forge an alliance among all universalists, whether religious or secular, against old and new forms of anti-universalism, such as an increasingly rampant anti-Islamism.

I have now set out what I believe to be four of the main intellectual challenges facing Christianity. Of course, this list is not exhaustive. I have limited myself to those challenges that relate to the core of the Christian message. This does not, so it seems to me, apply in the same way to those present-day processes of change that are closer to the realm of political issues. I have no wish to downplay the imperative of responding, to ecological hazards, the enormous dangers of unregulated financial markets, the problem of world hunger, or global power shifts. But these are tasks facing every contemporary intellectual school and value system, rather than challenges specific to the Christian faith. Some readers will be struck, however, by the fact that two points are missing from my list that many would expect to find at the top of it. I conclude by clarifying my reasons for omitting them.

First, I have chosen not to classify the problems of sexual morality as a key intellectual challenge. It seems plain to me that Christian teaching on this subject must glean all its principles from the ethos of love. It is only when people lose sight of this and derive teachings not from the ethos of love but from a dubious anthropology and a flawed conception of natural law that problems arise here. In the field of contraception, having children is then wrongly given precedence over the physical expression of love; in judging gay relationships, homosexuality is declared a problem rather than focusing once again on how the love between two human beings ought to be lived; and the meaning of priestly celibacy is easily misunderstood by outsiders because they perceive it as another symptom of hostility to the sexual sphere instead of an indication of a liberating asceticism, which some individuals choose to enter into voluntarily and uncoerced in order to devote themselves completely to serving others. I see no profound intellectual challenges here. All that is actually involved here is (at last) ensuring free expression of the core of the Christian message of love.

Also missing from my list is the challenge facing Christians as a result of the supposed "dictatorship of relativism" (Joseph Ratzinger, Pope Benedict XVI). Quite apart from the fact that the term "dictatorship" is very strong when we are dealing with the battle of public opinion and should not be used to attack a majority or hegemonic position—the term "relativism" is also a poor way to characterize the views that dominate in public life in general or the academic life of Western societies. Only a tiny number of people are explicitly committed to a relativist stance on epistemological or moral philosophical issues. It would be completely wrong to suggest that these represent a majority or even a defining, dictatorial minority. It would be more accurate to assume a pluralism of philosophical doctrines and pre-philosophical stances. What we find confronting each another are competing truth claims, and not, as a rule, a truth claim and its relativist negation. Today, the Catholic Church in particular has reason to grapple self-critically with a tradition of falsely understanding truth. Both in the Middle Ages and especially in the nineteenth and early twentieth centuries, the church often dealt with truth as if it were independent of individuals' experiences, as if it were located in a realm all its own, one administered and protected by the church, a realm to which individuals had obediently and compliantly to submit. But a contemporary post-totalitarian Christianity in the sense identified here is impossible if it fails to recognize the multiperspectival nature of all epistemic processes, not to mention the diversity of possible ways in which religious experiences can be expressed.

Particularly in the nineteenth century, the Catholic Church took the flawed approach of enshrining in law the understanding of faith as obedience to church doctrines. This entails understanding the church as what we might call a "quasi-state." It is a mistake for the simple reason that—in contrast to the state—people always have the option of leaving the church. As a quasi-state, the church is deficient in a "constitutional" sense as well: nontransparent, bureaucratically cumbersome, with no built-in protection of subjective rights and lacking mechanisms of organizational self-reform.[14] This flawed approach becomes particularly dangerous if institutional structures are linked with expectations of loyalty. Ernst-Wolfgang Böckenförde has persuasively argued that applying to the church a kind of "reason of state," or what we might call "reason of church," is responsible for the church's long history of failure in uncovering and prosecuting cases of abuse.[15] This amounts to the self-sacralization of an institution—when this institution ought to measure itself, in fact, and allow itself to be measured, against the aspiration to sacredness inherent in its conception of God. It thus runs the risk of being perceived as attractive for the wrong reasons—like "a magnificent ruin or an authenticated antique,"[16] rather than on account of its Christian message.

It seems to me that Christianity is fundamentally well-equipped to face each of the four challenges I have explored here. But it must abandon the defensive posture it has felt compelled to adopt or retreated to after decades of advancing secularization, mainly in Europe, and show that it is capable of articulating its message in new and convincing ways in light of these challenges. Only then can it avoid being perceived as an ultimately irrelevant moral authority. Philosophy and theology are necessary but not sufficient to such new articulation. The necessary rearticulation of what we mean by the sacred, transcendence, salvation, the prophets, or the Messiah cannot succeed without history and social sciences; without them, we shall be unable to understand what it means, in our world, to go beyond the dynamic of sacrifice through the self-sacrifice of a God who became flesh in human form.

Conclusion: Is Christianity Leaving Europe Behind?

"Those were beautiful, magnificent times, when Europe was a Christian land, when *one* Christianity dwelled on this civilized continent, and when *one* common interest joined the most distant provinces of this vast spiritual empire."[1] These are the famous opening lines of one of the most influential manifestos of early German Romanticism, namely, the 1799 fragment *Christianity or Europe* by Friedrich von Hardenberg, known as Novalis (the clearer of new land). This text was initially a lecture delivered in Jena in November of that year; it was decades before it was published (in 1826) under a title not chosen by Novalis.[2] Novalis's text embodies a very special, quite new understanding of past, present, and future. In the wistful tone of the fairy tale, Novalis bathes Europe's past in a golden light; as he looks back over history, it is above all the Middle Ages that appear as an era of homogeneous Christianity. The present, meanwhile, is presented highly critically in Novalis's text. For him, it is dominated by egotism and a suffocating rationalism; material interests hold sway. The main reason for Europe's dire condition and the losses it has suffered seems to be the secularization of Europe. Like Friedrich Schleiermacher's talks on religion, also from 1799, Novalis's work is one of the German intellectual responses to the French Revolution and its consequences for religious politics. The battle against religion is also responsible for new superstitions: "Where there are no gods, phantoms rule."[3] While Novalis paints a very gloomy picture of the present, the prospects for the future that he presents are bright indeed. He predicts the emergence of a supranational European state, held together by a renewed Christianity, which will overcome its confessional divisions; in a cosmopolitan spirit, rather than excluding other parts of the world, it will invite them to engage in peaceful cooperation. Novalis is keen to underline that this renewed Christianity must no longer be "sacrilegiously enclosed within the boundaries of the state,"[4] but should keep its distance from the interests of all states.

This is not the place to go into this text's multilayered effective history or its place in Novalis's oeuvre. It is no wonder that this text could be perceived as prophetic in a very different historical situation in Germany, namely, after the collapse of the Third Reich, when many people placed their hopes in the renewal of the Christian "Occident." In this discourse, however, there was no longer any sign of the cosmopolitan gesture of invitation to other parts of the world—quite the opposite. Now Christianity, European culture, and the "Occident" functioned mainly as terms of cultural and political exclusion—of Russia, Asia, the Orient, and often the United States as well. Even today this discourse flares up regularly, again under radically different historical conditions. This is why I now conclude this book by briefly asking how Novalis's three basic assumptions appear today and in light of the insights presented in this book. Was Europe ever homogeneously Christian? Is Europe today entirely secular? Does the future of Europe belong to a renewed Christianity—or, conversely, is Christianity leaving Europe?

It seems to me that we can answer the first question firmly in the negative. There are six reasons to reject the notion of a once homogeneously Christian Europe, and I shall run through them briefly now. No one now disputes the continuous significance of the Jewish religion in European history. But Islam, too, became a part of Europe long before the labor migration of the past few decades. In fact, mostly on the Iberian peninsula and in the Balkans, Islam has had a long European history. Further, in much of Northern and Eastern Europe especially, pre-Christian religious practices and ideas persisted into the late Middle Ages. Some countries, such as Lithuania, were Christianized only in the fourteenth century. Christianization from above, which is what generally took place, requires several generations to achieve broad effects. For a long time, the adoption of Christianity was molded by the specific pre-Christian religion of a given population, and in some cases this may still be the case. Ancient (primarily Greek and Roman) polytheisms did not have an impact on European religious and intellectual history on just one occasion, in the Renaissance,[5] but have repeatedly functioned as a potential source of inspiration or challenge. What is more, the notion of a uniform Christianity masks its internal heterogeneity. Since the Reformation and the division of the church to which it gave rise, it has been impossible to overlook the dramatic character of the relationship among differing forms of Christianity. Attempts were certainly made to defuse the clash between the confessions through religious peace settlements (such as those of 1555 and 1648); but given the limited size of the individual territories in the Empire, this only ever succeeded in a very partial way. More important in the present context is the fact that the Reformation was not the first historical event with the undesired consequence of pluralization. The division between Orthodox and Latin Christianity occurred centuries earlier. Furthermore, in the Middle Ages, the Latin Church was characterized by considerable internal diversity and was repeatedly caught up in conflicts with so-called heretical movements. And finally, the rise of the "secular option" (Charles Taylor), to which I have referred on a number of occasions in this book, in other words, the increasing potential for and availability of worldviews based on nonbelief, is a significant pluralizing step; to the extent that responses to new secular worldviews may themselves prompt new processes of sacralization or a new receptivity, for example, to Asian religious traditions, there is, again, more going on here than just secularization.

So we should view Europe as very rich in traditions of religious pluralism. If we also consider that the various religious traditions have not simply developed in hermetic isolation from one another but through frequent interaction—Christian mysticism is influenced by its Jewish counterpart, Francis of Assisi took some of his inspiration from his experience with Muslims—then the overall picture changes definitively.[6] In sum, Europe was never uniformly Christian—and Christianity, by the way, was never solely European. Enthusiasts for a Christian Occident easily overlook, not just the fact that the origins of Christianity lay outside Europe but also that its early spread occurred along a variety of routes, some of which led to the outermost fringes of Europe or away from Europe (Armenia, Georgia; the Copts; dissemination to India and even to China in the case of the Nestorians). It is no coincidence that in this age of the globalization of Christianity, people are becoming more aware of this forgotten or "lost" history.[7]

The second question, as to whether Europe is largely secular, can certainly be answered in the affirmative to a greater extent than in the time of Novalis or Schleiermacher. In retrospect, it is surprising how much contemporary commentators in parts of Europe around 1800 saw religion as on the defensive. The present-day situation is highly heterogeneous.[8] I discuss this in several chapters of the present book, particularly in light of whether Europe's enormous regional and national differences can be explained as a function of varying degrees of modernization. In chapter 1, I dispute this idea; in chapter 3, I put forward an alternative explanation of processes of secularization with reference to relevant examples. There is no need to repeat any of this here. What matters here, to sum things up, is that Europe today is indeed strongly secularized in certain countries, but this does not apply everywhere, and even in strongly secularized countries, with a few exceptions, large numbers of people belong to religious communities, share beliefs, and participate in religious practices and rituals at least occasionally, whether individually or collectively.

As far as the future is concerned, in chapter 9, I very cautiously make certain predictions. In particular, I emphasize the dissolution of religious milieus, but also the emergence of new ones, as well as the huge importance of migration to the religious situation in Europe. It goes without saying that religious revitalization in those post-Communist countries in which this is found (Russia, Romania) is of great importance. It is also important to acknowledge that the shattering of the idea that modernization inevitably leads to secularization opens up new possibilities for faith. But realization of these new possibilities depends on convincing action by the various believers and religious communities. In the foreseeable future, Europe's future will not belong to a renewed Christianity—even if this renewal does occur at some point. The future of Europe will be a multireligious one; it should also be characterized, and I hope to contribute to this with the present book, by a new open-mindedness on the part of both believers and nonbelievers, whenever they agree on the fundamental values of moral universalism.

Novalis's text is titled "Christianity or Europe." I would modify this today by stating that we can be (pro-)Europeans and Christians, but should reject attempts to fuse the two together. Such fusion results in an ideology of exclusion and misuses Christianity to further this ideology. It is characteristic, as for example in debates on Turkish accession to the European Union, that the people who highlight that Turkey is not Christian otherwise have very little time for the Christian message.[9] There may be many political and economic factors, which I am not concerned with here, that augur badly for Turkish accession. But there are no persuasive arguments against Turkish membership based on cultural, let alone religious factors. Those who share European values cannot be excluded for such reasons.[10]

This is also of great importance because the migrations of the past few decades have wrought major changes to Europe's religious landscape. We are by no means dealing here only with Muslim migrants but, to varying degrees in different European countries, also with Christian ones. They often bring with them a Christianity that has been gaining new adherents and growing in strength as a result of missionary work and colonization, but in recent decades chiefly through spontaneous dissemination. Ironically, in answering the question of whether Christianity is leaving Europe, it seems plausible to suggest that in important respects it is in fact arriving there! We cannot yet predict what the consequences of this unpredicted process will be for the religious situation in Europe. The possible future of Christianity is being determined by the interplay between Europe (and North America), on the one hand, and a globalized Christianity, on the other, and, just as important, by global political constellations that may inject conflict into the relationship between the followers of different religions. Conflict or dialogue between religions, a new de-Europeanization of Christianity, and the overcoming of old hostilities between believers and nonbelievers in favor of an opposition between universalists of all kinds and the (nationalist or racist) opponents of universalism: this seems to me to describe the situation in which faith today can be a living option.

Notes

FOREWORD

1. Charles Taylor, *A Secular Age* (Cambridge, MA: Belknap Press of Harvard University Press, 2007); reviewed in Hans Joas, "Die säkulare Option. Ihr Aufstieg und ihre Folgen," *Deutsche Zeitschrift für Philosophie* 57 (2009): 293–300.
2. Hans Joas, *The Sacredness of the Person: A New Genealogy of Human Rights* (Washington, DC: Georgetown University Press, 2013), 97–139. Of my writings on Troeltsch's religious theory, see here only Hans Joas, "Die Selbständigkeit religiöser Phänomene. Ernst Troeltsch als Vorbild der Religionsforschung," *Fuge. Journal für Religion und Moderne* 6 (2010): 15–28.

INTRODUCTION

1. I go into the various reasons in depth in "Society, State and Religion: Their Relationship from the Perspective of the World Religions," my introduction to *Secularization and the World Religions*, ed. Hans Joas and Klaus Wiegandt (Liverpool: Liverpool University Press, 2009), 1–22.
2. Charles Taylor, "The Polysemy of the Secular," *Social Research* 76, no. 4 (2009): 1163.
3. Many passages in the books I have co-authored with Wolfgang Knöbl indirectly perform this task: *Social Theory: Twenty Introductory Lectures* (Cambridge: Cambridge University Press, 2009); *War in Social Thought: Hobbes to the Present* (Princeton, NJ: Princeton University Press, 2012). For a more direct effort, see Hans Joas, "Gefährliche Prozessbegriffe. Eine Warnung vor der Rede von Differenzierung, Rationalisierung und Modernisierung," in *Umstrittene Säkularisierung. Soziologische und historische Analysen zur Differenzierung von Religion und Politik*, ed. Karl Gabriel et al. (Berlin: Berlin University Press, 2012), 603–22.
4. Ernst Troeltsch, "Das Wesen des modernen Geistes" (1907), in id., *Aufsätze zur Geistesgeschichte und Religionssoziologie* (Tübingen: Mohr, 1925), 328.

CHAPTER I

1. On the conceptual history of secularization, see Hermann Lübbe, *Säkularisierung. Geschichte eines ideenpolitischen Begriffs* (Freiburg: Karl Alber, 1965); Giacomo Marramao, *Die Säkularisierung der westlichen Welt* (Frankfurt am Main: Insel, 1996); Werner Conze, Hans Wolfgang Strätz, and Hermann Zabel, "Säkularisation, Säkularisierung," in vol. 5 of *Geschichtliche Grundbegriffe*, ed. Otto Brunner, Werner Conze, and Reinhart Koselleck (Stuttgart: Klett-Cotta, 1984), 789–829.

2. José Casanova, *Public Religions in the Modern World* (Chicago: University of Chicago Press, 1994). Charles Taylor's use of the term "secularization" in the sense of the rise of a secular option adds another variant.

3. Thomas Luckmann, *The Invisible Religion: The Problem of Religion in Modern Society* (New York: Macmillan, 1967).

4. See esp. chapter 5 of this book.

5. For a slightly polemical but brilliant and very useful article, see Rodney Stark, "Secularization, R.I.P.," *Sociology of Religion* 60 (1999): 249–73.

6. Quoted in a commentary on Henry Fielding, *Joseph Andrews' Abenteuer* (Berlin: Aufbau, 1974), 436. See also William H. Trapnell, *Thomas Woolston: Madman and Deist* (Bristol, UK: Thoemmes Press, 1994).

7. Lawrence Sterne, *The Life and Opinions of Tristram Shandy, Gentleman*, ed. Melvyn New and Joan New (Gainesville: University Presses of Florida, 1978), 2: 588–95.

8. See the quotation in Frederick the Great's last will and testament in Friedrich II, king of Prussia, *Die Politischen Testamente* (Berlin: Hobbing, 1922), 230. Remarkably, in his account of the Illuminati, Reinhart Koselleck (id., *Critique and Crisis: Enlightenment and the Pathogenesis of Modern Society* [Cambridge, MA: MIT Press, 1988], 133) sees precisely how a prediction of disappearance—in this case of the absolutist regime—can turn into a cunningly concealed weapon, because it allows one to avoid making explicit criticisms. But he does not relate this idea to the prediction of the disappearance of Christianity or religion. See Hans Joas, "The Contingency of Secularization: Reflections on the Problem of Secularization in the Work of Reinhart Koselleck," in *The Benefit of Broad Horizons: Intellectual and Institutional Preconditions for a Global Social Science. Festschrift for Björn Wittrock*, ed. Hans Joas and Barbro Klein (Leiden: Brill, 2010), 87–104.

9. Thomas Jefferson to Dr. Benjamin Waterhouse, June 26, 1822, in Saul Padover, ed., *The Complete Jefferson* (New York: Duell, Sloan & Pearce, 1943), 956. See also Johann N. Neem, "The Early Republic: Thomas Jefferson's Philosophy of History and the Future of American Christianity," in *Prophesies of Godlessness: Predictions of America's Imminent Secularization from the Puritans to the*

Present Day, ed. Charles Mathewes and Christopher McKnight Nichols (Oxford: Oxford University Press, 2008), 35–52. As far as I know there is no European equivalent of the latter volume that assesses the history of European predictions of secularization.

10. Manuel Borutta, "Genealogie der Säkularisierungstheorie. Zur Historisierung einer großen Erzählung der Moderne," *Geschichte und Gesellschaft* 36 (2010): 347–76; see also passages in Manuel Borutta, *Antikatholizismus. Deutschland und Italien im Zeitalter der Kulturkämpfe* (Göttingen: Vandenhoeck & Ruprecht, 2010).

11. *New York Times*, February 25, 1968. Berger later distanced himself from this assessment, of course: see Peter L. Berger, "Protestantism and the Quest for Certainty," *Christian Century*, August 26–September 2 (1998): 782–96. On Berger's assessment, see Hans Joas, *Do We Need Religion? On the Experience of Self-Transcendence* (Boulder, CO: Paradigm, 2007), 21–35.

12. Beginning with David Martin, "Towards Eliminating the Concept of Secularization," in *Penguin Survey of the Social Sciences*, ed. Julius Gould (London: Penguin Books, 1965), 169–82, through Martin, *A General Theory of Secularization* (Oxford: Blackwell, 1978), to his two important later essay collections, *On Secularization: Towards a Revised General Theory* (Burlington, VT: Ashgate, 2005) and *The Future of Christianity. Reflections on Violence and Democracy, Religion and Secularization* (Burlington, VT: Ashgate, 2011).

13. Karl Marx, *Critique of Hegel's Philosophy of Right* (Cambridge: CUP Archive, 1977), 131.

14. Hans Joas, *The Genesis of Values* (Chicago: University of Chicago Press, 2000) and *Do We Need Religion?*

15. Hans Joas, "The Religious Situation in the U.S.A.," in *Secularization*, ed. Joas and Wiegandt, 229–40; and in an expanded version on the basis of the Bertelsmann Religion Monitor, Hans Joas, "The Religious Situation in the United States," in *What the World Believes: Analyses and Commentary on the Religion Monitor 2008*, ed. Bertelsmann-Stiftung (Gütersloh: Bertelsmann, 2009), 317–34. These also provide further references of relevance to the claims put forward here.

16. Roger Finke and Rodney Stark, *The Churching of America, 1776–1990* (New Brunswick, NJ: Rutgers University Press, 1992).

17. For an outstanding survey of the global religious history of the nineteenth century, see C. A. Baily, *The Birth of the Modern World, 1780–1914* (Oxford: Blackwell, 2004), 325–65. With particular emphasis on the political dimension, see also Jürgen Osterhammel, *Die Verwandlung der Welt. Eine Geschichte des 19. Jahrhunderts* (Munich: Beck, 2009), 1239–78.

18. In their *Einführung in die Religionswissenschaft* (Munich: Beck, 2003) Hans Gerhard Kippenberg and Kocku von Stuckrad devote an entire chapter to this topic with reference to Hinduism (37–48).

19. For an overview, see David Martin, "The Relevance of the European Model of Secularization in Latin America and Africa," in *Secularization*, ed. Joas and Wiegandt, 278–95, and Joachim Gentz, "The Religious Situation in East Asia," ibid., 241–77.

20. To quote the title of the famous novel by Carlo Levi on the period of his banishment to southern Italy in the 1930s, *Christ Stopped at Eboli* (first published in 1945; English trans., Harmondsworth, UK: Penguin Books, 1982).

21. For a nuanced account that critically examines Levi, see Wolfgang Reinhard, *Lebensformen Europas. Eine historische Kulturanthropologie* (Munich: Beck, 2004), 551–80.

22. See chapter 3 of this book.

CHAPTER 2

1. William James, *The Varieties of Religious Experience* (1902; Cambridge, MA: Harvard University Press, 1985).

2. See Joas, *Genesis of Values* (which includes an interpretation of James's *Varieties of Religious Experience*, 35–53) and *Do We Need Religion?*

3. Hans Joas, *Sacredness of the Person*, esp. 54ff.

4. For extensive quantitative data, see Hans Joas and Wolfgang Knöbl, eds., *Gewalt in den USA* (Frankfurt am Main: Fischer, 1994).

5. Phil Zuckerman, *Society without God: What the Least Religious Nations Can Tell Us about Contentment* (New York: New York University Press, 2008), 17–18.

6. Ibid., 193n55, with reference to Gregory Paul, "Cross-National Correlations of Quantifiable Societal Health with Popular Religiosity and Secularism in the Prosperous Democracies," *Journal of Religion and Society* 7 (2005): 1–17. A good overview can be found in Bernhard Spilka et al., *The Psychology of Religion: An Empirical Approach* (New York: Guilford, 2009), esp. 416–79.

7. See the remarks in Callum Brown, *The Death of Christian Britain: Understanding Secularization, 1800–2000* (London: Routledge, 2001), 195ff.

8. Andrew Greeley, "Protestant and Catholic: Is the Analogical Imagination Extinct?" *American Sociological Review* 54 (1989): 485–502.

9. Ibid., 487.

10. Ibid., 493.

11. Walter Sinnott-Armstrong, *Morality without God?* (Oxford: Oxford University Press, 2009), xviii.

12. Ernst Troeltsch, "Atheistische Ethik" (1895), in id., *Gesammelte Schriften* (Tübingen: Mohr, 1912), 2: 525–55.

13. See Pew Forum on Religion and Public Life, *U.S. Religious Landscape Survey 2009* (Washington, D.C.: Pew Forum, 2009), chap. 2, 30.

14. Bronislaw Malinowski, *Crime and Custom in Savage Society* (London: Kegan Paul, 1926). For an outstanding attempt to tackle these issues in more depth, see Marshall Sahlins, *Stone Age Economics* (New York: Aldine de Gruyter, 1972).

15. Ibid., 9.

16. Ibid., 18.

17. Ibid., 20–21.

18. Ibid., 23.

19. Emile Durkheim, *The Division of Labour in Society* (1893; Basingstoke, UK: Macmillan, 1984).

20. Malinowski, *Crime and Custom*, 67–68.

21. Marcel Mauss, *The Gift* (1923; London: Routledge, 2002); Marcel Hénaff, *The Price of Truth: Gift, Money, and Philosophy* (Stanford, CA: Stanford University Press, 2010).

22. See, e.g., Jean Piaget, *The Moral Judgement of the Child* (1932; Harmondsworth, UK: Penguin Books, 1977); Lawrence Kohlberg, "Stage and Sequence: The Cognitive-Developmental Approach to Socialization," in *Handbook of Socialization Theory and Research*, ed. David A. Goslin (Chicago: Rand McNally, 1969), 347–480.

23. Joas and Knöbl, *Social Theory*, 94–122.

24. See Joas, *Sacredness of the Person*

25. Nikolai Leskov, *On the Edge of the World* (Crestwood, N.Y.: St. Vladimir's Seminary Press, 1993).

26. See Robert Bellah, "Religious Pluralism and Religious Truth," in *The Robert Bellah Reader*, ed. Robert Bellah and Steve Tipton (Durham, NC: Duke University Press, 2006), 481. For a penetrating account of the Christian understanding of reciprocity, see Heinrich Bedford-Strohm, *Gemeinschaft aus kommunikativer Freiheit* (Gütersloh: Gütersloher Verlagshaus, 1999), esp. 237–84.

27. Joas, *Genesis of Values*, 161–86.

28. Karl Jaspers, *The Origin and Goal of History* (1949; English trans., 1953; London: Routledge, 2011). There is more on this thesis of a fundamental shift in religious history between 800 and 200 BC in later chapters of this book, esp. chapters 8 and 10.

CHAPTER 3

1. Owen Chadwick, *The Secularization of the European Mind in the 19th Century* (Cambridge: Cambridge University Press, 1975), 159–60.

2. See, e.g., Joas, "Society, State and Religion," 1–22.

3. Grace Davie, *Religion in Modern Europe: A Memory Mutates* (Oxford: Oxford University Press, 2000).

4. Anders Bäckström and Grace Davie, "A Preliminary Conclusion: Gathering the Threads and Moving on," in vol 1. of *Welfare and Religion in 21st Century Europe*, ed. Anders Bäckström and Grace Davie (Burlington, VT: Ashgate, 2010), 191.

5. Kevin Christiano, "Clio Goes to Church: Revisiting and Revitalizing Historical Thinking in the Sociology of Religion," *Sociology of Religion* 69 (2008): 20.

6. Anthony J. Carroll S.J., *Protestant Modernity. Weber, Secularization and Protestantism* (Scranton, PA: University of Scranton Press, 2007); see also my review, *Journal of Religion* 90 (2010): 445–47; for my critique of Weber in this respect, see Hans Joas, "The Axial Age Debate as Religious Discourse," in *The Axial Age and Its Consequences*, ed. Robert Bellah and Hans Joas (Cambridge, MA: Belknap Press of Harvard University Press, 2012), 9–29.

7. See esp. Christian Smith, "Introduction: Rethinking the Secularization of American Public Life," in id., ed., *The Secular Revolution: Power, Interests, and Conflict in the Secularization of American Public Life* (Berkeley: University of California Press, 2003), 1–96.

8. Taylor, *Secular Age* On "vectors," see ibid., 786n92; on the "nova effect," 299ff.

9. Marcel Reinhard, *Paris pendant la Révolution* (Paris: Centre de documentation universitaire, 1966), 1: 196, quoted in Hugh McLeod, *Religion and the People of Western Europe, 1789–1989* (Oxford: Oxford University Press, 1997²), 1. I draw here on the ideas presented in my book *The Sacredness of the Person* (Washington, DC: Georgetown University Press 2013), 11ff.

10. Timothy Tackett, "The French Revolution and Religion to 1794," in *Enlightenment, Reawakening and Revolution, 1660–1815* (= *The Cambridge History of Christianity*, vol. 7), ed. Stewart J. Brown and Timothy Tackett (Cambridge: Cambridge University Press, 2006), 550.

11. Ibid., 536.

12. Quotations in ibid., 556.

13. Alexis de Tocqueville, *The Ancien Régime and the Revolution* (1856; London: Penguin Books, 2008), e.g., 23.

14. Hugh McLeod, *Piety and Poverty. Working-Class Religion in Berlin, London and New York, 1870–1914* (New York: Holmes & Meier, 1996); Hugh McLeod, *Secularization in Western Europe, 1848–1914* (New York: St. Martin's Press, 2000). My remarks have also been significantly influenced by Franz Schnabel, *Deutsche Geschichte im neunzehnten Jahrhundert.* vol. 4: *Die religiösen Kräfte* (1937; Munich: DTV, 1987); Thomas Nipperdey, *Deutsche Geschichte, 1800–1918* (Munich: Beck, 1983–92); Olaf Blaschke, "Das 19. Jahrhundert. Ein zweites konfessionelles Zeitalter?" *Geschichte und Gesellschaft* 26 (2000): 38–75; and Lucian Hölscher, "Die Religion des Bürgers. Bürgerliche Frömmigkeit und protestantische Kirche im 19. Jahrhundert," *Historische Zeitschrift* 250 (1990): 595–629.

15. Timothy Leary, quoted in Hugh McLeod, *The Religious Crisis of the 1960s* (Oxford: Oxford University Press, 2007), 131.

16. In his book on the 1960s and in his writings in general, Hugh McLeod seems to me to downplay the differences between Europe and the United States. This is one of the few things I disagree with him about. My impression is that his views on Europe are a bit one-sided, because his analyses focus on Great Britain, which has probably caused him to underestimate the divergence between Europe and America.

17. Bernard Yack, *The Fetishism of Modernities: Epochal Self-Consciousness in Contemporary Social and Political Thought* (Notre Dame, IN: University of Notre Dame Press, 1997). See the following chapters of this book.

18. On "pacification" and its preconditions, see Joas and Knöbl, *War in Social Thought*, and Hans Joas, "Peace through Democracy?" *European Journal of Social Theory* 15 (2012): 21–34.

19. Max Scheler, *On the Eternal in Man* (1923; New Brunswick, NJ: Transaction, 2010), 122–23.

CHAPTER 4

1. Ernst Troeltsch, "Das Verhältnis des Protestantismus zur Kultur. Überblick," originally in *Religion in Geschichte und Gegenwart*, vol. 4 (1913), cols. 1912–20; cited here from id., *Gesammelte Schriften*, vol. 4 (Tübingen, 1925), 191.

2. Ibid., 192.

3. Ibid.

4. Ibid., 195–96.

5. Charles Taylor, *Sources of the Self* (Cambridge, MA: Harvard University Press, 1989), 211 and 224.

6. Georg Jellinek, *The Declarations of the Rights of Man and of Citizens: A Contribution to Modern Constitutional History* (1895; trans., New York: Holt, 1901); see also Hans Joas, "Max Weber and the Origins of Human Rights," in *Max Weber's Economy and Society: A Critical Companion*, ed. Charles Camic, Philip Gorski and David Trubek (Stanford, CA: Stanford University Press, 2005), 366–82.

7. Max Weber, *The Protestant Ethic and the Spirit of Capitalism* (1904) (New York: Oxford University Press, 2011); the form of words given here is from Troeltsch, "Verhältnis des Protestantismus zur Kultur," 200.

8. Otto Hintze, *Die Hohenzollern und ihr Werk* (Berlin: Parey, 1915).

9. For more detail, see Troeltsch in many of his works, esp. *Kritische Gesamtausgabe*, vol. 8: *Schriften zur Bedeutung des Protestantismus für die moderne Welt, 1906–1913* (Berlin: De Gruyter, 2001).

10. Robert K. Merton, *Science, Technology and Society in Seventeenth-Century England* (1938; New York: Howard Fertig, 1970); id., "Puritanism, Pietism, and Science," *Sociological Review* 28 (1936): 1–30.

11. Ralph Barton Perry, *Puritanism and Democracy* (New York: Vanguard, 1944).

12. See Marianne Weber, *Max Weber: A Biography* (New York: Wiley, 1975), 473.

13. Marcel Gauchet, *La révolution des droits de l'homme* (Paris: Gallimard, 1989), 14.

14. Sidney Hook, *Reason, Social Myths and Democracy* (New York: John Day, 1940), 76.

15. Philip S. Gorski, *The Disciplinary Revolution. Calvinism and the Rise of the State in Early Modern Europe* (Chicago: University of Chicago Press, 2003).

16. See Friedrich Wilhelm Graf, "Protestantism," in *Secularization and the World Religions*, ed. Joas and Wiegandt, 46–76.

17. Ernst Troeltsch, *The Social Teaching of the Christian Churches* (1912; London: Allen & Unwin, 1950), 673.

18. John O'Malley, *Trent and All That: Renaming Catholicism in the Early Modern Era* (Cambridge, MA: Harvard University Press, 2000), 122.

19. Robert Bellah, *Tokugawa Religion: The Cultural Roots of Modern Japan* (New York: Free Press, 1957).

20. Wolfgang Reinhard, "Historiker, 'Modernisierung' und Modernisierung. Erfahrungen mit dem Konzept 'Modernisierung' in der neueren Geschichte," in *Innovation und Originalität*, ed. Walter Haug and Burghart Wachinger (Tübingen: Niemeyer, 1993), 68.

21. Despite his admiration for the church as "complexio oppositorum": Carl Schmitt, *Roman Catholicism and Political Form* (1923; Westport, CT: Greenwood Press, 1996).

22. This is superbly demonstrated by Carroll, *Protestant Modernity*. See my review in *Journal of Religion* 90 (2010): 445–47.

23. On the following, see Hans Joas, "The Gift of Life. Parsons' Late Sociology of Religion," *Journal of Classical Sociology 1* (2001), 127–41.

24. Talcott Parsons, "Christianity," in id., *Action Theory and the Human Condition* (New York: Free Press, 1978), 173–74.

25. Ibid., 192.

26. Talcott Parsons, "Religion in Postindustrial America," in id., *Action Theory*, 308.

27. I am aware how ambiguous this concept is. For hugely valuable clarification, see Friedrich Wilhelm Graf, "Kulturprotestantismus. Zur Begriffsgeschichte einer theologiepolitischen Chiffre," in *Kulturprotestantismus. Beiträge zu einer Gestalt des modernen Christentums*, ed. Hans Martin Müller (Gütersloh: Mohn, 1992), 21–77.

28. Robert Bellah, *Religion in Human Evolution* (Cambridge, MA: Belknap Press of Harvard University Press, 2011), e.g., 267.

29. See chapter 9 of this book.

CHAPTER 5

1. See Ulrich Beck, *Risk Society: Towards a New Modernity* (1986; trans., Newbury Park, CA: Sage, 1992). See also my review, "Das Risiko der Gegenwartsdiagnosc," *Soziologische Revue* 11 (1988): 1–6.

2. See Wolfgang Knöbl, *Spielräume der Modernisierung. Das Ende der Eindeutigkeit* (Weilerswist: Velbrück, 2001).

3. See Yack, *Fetishism of Modernities.*

4. The leading American sociologist Daniel Bell was an early and important exception to the tendency to present an overly uniform picture of modernity and modernization. He underlined that societies are "radically disjunctive" and that the developmental patterns of social structure and culture are generally out of sync. He rejected the concept of secularization as hopelessly confused, along with the idea that we might transform a logical dichotomy such as modern/premodern into an explanatory schema for historical accounts. See Daniel Bell, "The Return of the Sacred?" in id., *The Winding Passage: Essays and Sociological Journeys 1960–1980* (Cambridge, MA: Abt Books, 1980), 324–54.

5. See Hans Joas, *The Creativity of Action* (Chicago: University of Chicago Press, 1996).

6. I have already attempted to do this in a number of publications. See ibid.; Hans Joas, "Globalisierung und Wertentstehung—Oder: 'Warum Marx und Engels doch nicht recht hatten,'" *Berliner Journal für Soziologie* 8 (1998): 329–32; and recently also Joas, "Gefährliche Prozessbegriffe."

7. Richard Rorty, "Failed Prophecies, Glorious Hopes," in id., *Philosophy and Social Hope* (London: Penguin Books, 1999), 202–9.

8. Eric Hobsbawm, *The Age of Capital, 1848–1875* (London: Weidenfeld & Nicolson, 1975), 237.

9. See Albert Hirschman, *The Passions and the Interests: Political Arguments for Capitalism before Its Triumph* (Princeton, NJ: Princeton University Press, 1977).

10. See Stephen Toulmin, *Cosmopolis: The Hidden Agenda of Modernity* (New York: Free Press, 1990).

11. William James quoted in Gerald Myers, *William James: His Life and Thought* (New Haven, CT: Yale University Press, 1986), 43.

12. See Joas, *Creativity of Action*, 223–44.

13. See Jacob Burckhardt, *Reflections on History* (1905 [written 1868]; London: Allen & Unwin, 1943).

14. See Randall Collins, *Macrohistory: Essays in Sociology of the Long Run* (Stanford, CA: Stanford University Press, 1999), 152–75.

15. See Joas, *Do We Need Religion?* 32–49.

16. See Ernst Troeltsch, "Die Bedeutung des Begriffs der Kontingenz" (1910), in id., *Gesammelte Schriften* (Tübingen: Mohr, 1922), 2: 769–78.

17. An important study of this thematic complex has now been produced by Peter Vogt, *Kontingenz und Zufall. Eine Ideen- und Begriffsgeschichte* (Berlin: Akademie, 2011). See also my foreword (11–16).

18. See John Dewey, *The Quest for Certainty* (London: Allen & Unwin, 1929).

19. See Pippa Norris and Ronald Inglehart, *Sacred and Secular: Religion and Politics Worldwide* (Cambridge: Cambridge University Press, 2004). See the outstanding critique by Daniel Silver, "Religion without Instrumentalization," *Archives européennes de sociologie* 47 (2006): 421–34.

20. See Jean-François Lyotard, *The Postmodern Condition: A Report on Knowledge* (Minneapolis: University of Minnesota Press, 1984).

CHAPTER 6

1. Thomas Bender, *Community and Social Change in America* (New Brunswick, NJ: Rutgers University Press, 1978), 46.

2. Richard Sennett, *The Corrosion of Character: The Personal Consequences of Work in the New Capitalism* (New York: Norton, 1998), 10.

3. Ibid.

4. Ibid., 117.

5. See Rainer Lepsius, "Parteiensystem und Sozialstruktur. Zum Problem der Demokratisierung der deutschen Gesellschaft" (1966), reprinted in id., *Demokratie in Deutschland* (Göttingen: Vandenhoeck & Ruprecht, 1993), 25–50. For more detail, see Hans Joas and Frank Adloff, "Transformations of German Civil Society: Milieu Change and Community Spirit," in *Civil Society. Berlin Perspectives*, ed. John Keane (New York: Berghahn, 2006), 103–38.

6. Wilhelm Heitmeyer, "Das Desintegrationstheorem. Ein Erklärungsansatz zu fremdenfeindlich motivierter rechtsextremistischer Gewalt und zur Lähmung gesellschaftlicher Institutionen," in *Das Gewaltdilemma*, ed. Wilhelm Heitmeyer (Frankfurt am Main: Suhrkamp, 1994), 46.

7. Some reflections on this in Hans Joas, "Kontingenzbewusstsein. Der Erste Weltkrieg und der Bruch im Zeitbewusstsein der Moderne," in *Aggression und Katharsis. Der Erste Weltkrieg im Diskurs der Moderne*, ed. Petra Ernst et al. (Vienna: Passagen, 2004), 43–56.

8. Joas, *Genesis of Values*.

9. E. W. Burgess, *The Family: From Institution to Companionship* (New York: American Book Co., 1945).

10. Talcott Parsons, "Comparative Studies and Evolutionary Change," in id., *Social Systems and the Evolution of Action Theory* (New York: Free Press, 1977), 279–320, esp. 307ff. For more depth, see Joas, *Sacredness of the Person*, 173ff.

11. Sennett, *Corrosion of Character*, 58.

12. On the resulting consequences for value transmission, see Joas, *Do We Need Religion?*, 31–33.

13. Beck, *Risk Society*; Peter Gross, *Die Multioptionsgesellschaft* (Frankfurt am Main: Suhrkamp, 1994). Both authors have addressed the topic of religion in later publications: Ulrich Beck, *A God of One's Own: Religion's Capacity for Peace and Potential for Violence* (Cambridge: Polity Press, 2010); Peter Gross, *Jenseits der Erlösung. Die Wiederkehr der Religion und die Zukunft des Christentums* (Bielefeld: Transcript, 2007). It is to Gross's credit that he refrains from asking sweeping questions about the future of religion per se, focusing instead on the future of salvation religions; his vision is of a "relaxed religiosity" without the prospect of otherworldly or innerworldly redemption. For a critique, see my review, Hans Joas, "Ohne einen Finger zu krümmen, sind wir erlöst," *Frankfurter Allgemeine Zeitung*, May 9, 2008, 41.

14. See the list provided in Karel Dobbelaere, *Secularization: An Analysis at Three Levels* (Brussels: Peter Lang, 2002), 173ff.

15. Of Berger's many works, I shall mention just Peter L. Berger, *A Far Glory: The Quest for Faith in an Age of Credulity* (New York: Free Press, 1992).

16. For my critique, see Joas, *Do We Need Religion?* 21–36. Sharp criticism of the use of the terms preference and choice with respect to religion can be found in Joshua Mitchell, "Religion Is Not a Preference," *Journal of Politics* 69 (2007): 351–62; the same issue includes a riposte by Clyde Wilcox et al., "Religious Preferences and Social Science. A Second Look," ibid., 874–79, and a reply by Joshua Mitchell, ibid., 880–83.

17. Taylor, *Secular Age*, 832n19.

18. The distinction between "living" and "dead" options is central to William James's analysis of the preconditions for faith, see id., *The Will to Believe* (1896; London: Longmans, 1905), 3.

CHAPTER 7

1. On the following understanding of religion, faith and values, see Joas, *Do We Need Religion?* and *Genesis of Values*.

2. George Santayana, "Reason in Religion," in vol. 4 of id., *Works* (New York: Scribner's, 1936), 4.

3. Wolfgang Huber, "The Judeo-Christian Tradition," in *The Cultural Values of Europe*, ed. Hans Joas and Klaus Wiegandt (Liverpool: Liverpool University Press, 2008), 43–59.

4. Rémi Brague, "Schluss mit den 'drei Monotheismen'!" *Communio* 2 (2007): 98–113.

5. Max Scheler, "Man in an Era of Adjustment" (1927), in id., *Philosophical Perspectives* (Boston: Beacon Press, 1958), 94–126.

6. It seems to me that this is a feature common to Max Weber's research program and the American pragmatists.

7. See Bellah, "Religious Pluralism and Religious Truth," 488.

8. This is the argument put forward by W. G. Runciman, "The Diffusion of Christianity in the Third Century AD as a Case-Study in the Theory of Cultural Selection," *European Journal of Sociology* 45 (2004): 3–21. For an overview of competing explanations, see Christoph Markschies, *Warum hat das Christentum in der Antike überlebt? Ein Beitrag zum Gespräch zwischen Kirchengeschichte und Systematischer Theologie* (Leipzig: Evangelische Verlagsanstalt, 2004 [Forum Theologische Literaturzeitung]).

9. On the issue of violence, see chapter 8 of this book.

10. For an excellent discussion, see Ernst Troeltsch, "Political Ethics and Christianity," in id., *Religion in History* (Minneapolis, MN: Fortress Press, 1997), 173–209.

CHAPTER 8

1. Karlheinz Deschner, *Kriminalgeschichte des Christentums* (Reinbek: Rowohlt, 1986–2013).

2. See Max Weber, *Economy and Society* (Berkeley: University of California Press, 1979), 399.

3. See Hans Joas, *War and Modernity* (Cambridge: Polity Press, 2003), 187–96.

4. See Rudolf Otto, *The Idea of the Holy* (1917; Oxford: Oxford University Press, 1950).

5. See Emile Durkheim, *The Elementary Forms of the Religious Life* (1912; Oxford: Oxford University Press, 2001).

6. On this and other mythologizations of violence, see Joas and Knöbl, *War in Social Thought*.

7. See Joas, *War and Modernity*, 111–21.

8. See René Girard, *Violence and the Sacred* (Baltimore, MD: Johns Hopkins University Press, 1977).

9. See Robert N. Bellah and Hans Joas, eds., *The Axial Age and Its Consequences* (Cambridge, MA: Belknap Press of Harvard University Press, 2012).

10. See, e.g., Jan Assmann, *The Price of Monotheism* (Stanford, CA: Stanford University Press, 2009). The thesis is much older, of course; it can be found in the work of David Hume in the eighteenth century.

11. See Joas, *War and Modernity*, 21–23 and 152–57.

12. Rolf Schieder, *Sind Religionen gefährlich?* (Berlin: Berlin University Press, 2008), 88.

13. Arnold Angenendt, *Toleranz und Gewalt. Das Christentum zwischen Bibel und Schwert* (Münster: Aschendorff, 2008).

14. See Knud Krakau, *Missionsbewusstsein und Völkerrechtsdoktrin in den Vereinigten Staaten von Amerika* (Frankfurt am Main: Metzner, 1967); Knud Krakau, "American Foreign Relations: A National Style?" *Diplomatic History* 8 (1984): 253–72.

15. Wolfgang Huber, "Religion, Politik und Gewalt in der heutigen Welt," in *Weltreligionen. Verstehen, Verständigung, Verantwortung,* ed. Karl Kardinal Lehmann (Frankfurt am Main: Verlag der Weltreligionen, 2009), 247.

16. See Reinhard, "Historiker, 'Modernisierung' und Modernisierung"; Horst Dreier, "Kanonistik und Konfessionalisierung—Marksteine auf dem Weg zum Staat," in *Artibus ingenuis,* ed. Georg Siebeck (Tübingen: Mohr, 2001), 133–69; José Casanova, *Europas Angst vor der Religion* (Berlin: Berlin University Press, 2009).

17. Jellinek, *Declarations of the Rights of Man and of Citizens.*

18. See Joas, "Max Weber and the Origins of Human Rights." On the various Protestantism theses, see chapter 4 of this book.

19. See Brian J. Grimm and Roger Finke, "Religious Persecution in Cross-National Context: Clashing Civilizations or Regulated Religious Economies?" *American Sociological Review* 72 (2007), 633–58.

20. See, e.g., Andreas Hasenclever, "Getting Religion Right. Zur Rolle von Religionen in politischen Konflikten," in *Religion und globale Entwicklung,* ed. Jürgen Willhelm and Hartmut Ihne (Berlin: Berlin University Press, 2009), 170–86. R. Scott Appleby, *The Ambivalence of the Sacred: Religion, Violence, and Reconciliation* (Lanham, MD: Rowman & Littlefield, 2000), presents important American research.

21. See Joas, "Peace through Democracy?"

22. See Dieter Senghaas, "The Realities of Cultural Struggles," in *Cultural Values of Europe,* ed. Joas and Wiegandt, 320–37. This excellent essay takes stock of criticisms of Samuel Huntington, *The Clash of Civilizations?* (Washington, DC: American Enterprise Institute, 1992).

23. Michael Geyer and Charles Bright, "Global Violence and Nationalizing Wars in Eurasia and America: The Geopolitics of War in the Mid Nineteenth-Century," *Comparative Studies in Society and History* 38 (1996): 624.

24. See Hans Gerhard Kippenberg, *Violence as Worship: Religious Wars in the Age of Globalization,* (Stanford, CA: Stanford University Press, 2011). For a synopsis of his argument, see also Hans Gerhard Kippenberg, "Zur Kontingenz religiösen Gewalthandelns," in *Handlung und Erfahrung. Das Erbe von Historismus und Pragmatismus und die Zukunft der Sozialtheorie,* ed. Bettina Hollstein et al. (Frankfurt am Main: Campus, 2011), 191–216.

25. Kippenberg, *Violence as Worship,* 211.

CHAPTER 9

1. David Martin, "Secularization and the Future of Christianity," *Journal of Contemporary Religion* 20 (2005): 145–60; a revised version is now available in Martin, *Future of Christianity*, 25–44.

2. See chapter 1 of this book.

3. Christof Wolf, "Religiöse Sozialization, konfessionelle Milieus und Generation," *Zeitschrift für Soziologie* 24 (1995): 345–57.

4. For more in-depth treatment of these issues, see Joas and Adloff, "Transformations of German Civil Society." I would like to stress that the term "social milieu" as I use it is geared towards actual social cohesion in contrast to its usage in market research, which refers merely to common ground or similarities in value orientations. Regrettably, the market research perspective has taken hold even in research on religion.

5. Lepsius, "Parteiensystem und Sozialstruktur."

6. Robert Wuthnow, *The Restructuring of American Religion* (Princeton, NJ: Princeton University Press, 1988).

7. Robert Putnam and David Campbell, *American Grace: How Religion Divides and Unites Us* (New York: Simon & Schuster, 2010).

8. Detlef Pollack, *Säkularisierung—ein moderner Mythos?* (Tübingen: Mohr, 2003), 10–11.

9. Eric Voegelin, *Political Religions* (1938; Lewiston, NY: E. Mellen, 1985).

10. Norris and Inglehart, *Sacred and Secular*

11. See chapter 3 of this book, "Waves of Secularization."

12. Of the extensive literature, I shall mention just Daniella Kane and Jung Mee Park, "The Puzzle of Korean Christianity: Geopolitical Networks and Religious Conversion in Early Twentieth-Century East Asia," *American Journal of Sociology* 115 (2009): 365–404, and David Martin, "Pentecostalism: Transnational Voluntarism in the Global Religious Economy," in id., *The Future of Christianity*, 63–84. For a focus on the role of social movements, see also Jin-Wook Shin, *Modernisierung und Zivilgesellschaft in Südkorea* (Berlin: Deutscher Universitätsverlag, 2005 (with a foreword by Hans Joas).

13. According to Ian Johnson, "China Gets Religion!" *New York Review of Books*, 22 December 2011, 55–58. This is the source of some of the following quantitative data. See also Gentz, "Religious Situation in East Asia."

14. Martin, "European Model of Secularization."

15. Elizabeth Brusco, *The Reformation of Machismo* (Austin: University of Texas Press, 1995).

16. For many of these observations, I am indebted to Philip Jenkins, *The Next Christendom: The Coming of Global Christianity* (Oxford: Oxford University Press, 2004).

17. Nancy Foner and Richard Alba, "Immigrant Religion in the U.S. and Western Europe: Bridge or Barrier to Inclusion?" *International Migration Review* 42 (2008): 360–92, is highly instructive in this respect. Astonishingly little research has been done in Germany on Christian migrant communities. One example is Karsten Lehmann, "Community-Kirchen im Wandel. Zur Entwicklung christlicher Migrantengemeinden zwischen 1950 und 2000," *Berliner Journal für Soziologie* 16 (2006): 485–501.

18. Kwame Bediako, *Christianity in Africa: The Renewal of a Non-Western Religion* (Maryknoll, NY: Orbis Books, 1995).

19. Franz-Xaver Kaufmann, "Zwischenräume und Wechselwirkungen. Der Verlust der Zentralperspektive und das Christentum," *Theologie und Glaube* 96 (2006): 309–23.

20. See chapter 7, and, with regard to the new constellation, the introduction to this book.

CHAPTER 10

1. Ernst Troeltsch, "Die Zukunftsmöglichkeiten des Christentums," *Logos* 1 (1910–11): 165–85 at 168.

2. Ernst Troeltsch, *Die Soziallehren der christlichen Kirchen und Gruppen* (Tübingen, 1912). Trans. as *The Social Teaching of the Christian Churches* (1931), in which see esp. 991–1013.

3. Robert Bellah et al., *Habits of the Heart: Individualism and Commitment in American Life* (Berkeley: University of California Press, 1985).

4. See Joas, *Creativity of Action*, 252ff.

5. See Paul Ricœur, "Love and Justice," in id., *Figuring the Sacred: Religion, Narrative and Imagination* (Minneapolis, MN: Fortress Press, 1995), 315–29; Joas, *Genesis of Values*, 169ff.

6. For an excellent account, see Matthias Jung, *Der bewusste Ausdruck. Anthropologie der Artikulation* (Berlin: De Gruyter, 2009).

7. For a study of this topic, see Joas, *Sacredness of the Person*.

8. Cardinal Karl Lehmann, "Catholic Christianity," in *Secularization*, ed. Joas and Wiegandt, 23–45.

9. Taylor, *Secular Age*, 282.

10. Troeltsch, "Zukunftsmöglichkeiten," 181.

11. More than any other contemporary thinker, Charles Taylor has contributed here to the structuring of contemporary conceptual alternatives and to the formulation of a Christian "incarnated Humanism." See Taylor, *Secular Age*, 618ff.

12. Jaspers, *Origin and Goal of History*; for Weber, see my chapter in Bellah and Joas, eds., *Axial Age*, 9–29.

13. The work of Shmuel Eisenstadt and Robert Bellah is especially relevant here. See, e.g., Shmuel Eisenstadt, "The Axial Age in World History," in *Cultural Values of Europe*, ed. Joas and Wiegandt, 22–42; Robert N. Bellah, "What Is Axial about the Axial Age?" *European Journal of Sociology* 46 (2005): 69–90. And see esp. Bellah, *Religion in Human Evolution*, and Bellah and Joas, eds., *Axial Age*.

14. Franz Xaver Kaufmann, *Kirchenkrise. Wie überlebt das Christentum?* (Freiburg: Herder, 2011).

15. Ernst-Wolfgang Böckenförde, "Das unselige Handeln nach Kirchenraison," *Süddeutsche Zeitung*, April 29, 2010, 2.

16. Schmitt, *Roman Catholicism and Political Form*, 12.

CONCLUSION

1. Novalis, "Christianity or Europe: A Fragment" (1799), in *The Early Political Writings of the German Romantics*, ed. Frederick C. Beiser (Cambridge: Cambridge University Press, 1996), 61.

2. See Wolfgang Braungart, "Subjekt Europa, Europas Subjekt. Novalis' katholische Provokation. Die Christenheit oder Europa," *Sinn und Form* 63 (2011): 546.

3. Novalis, "Christianity or Europe," 75.

4. Ibid., 66.

5. Hans Gerhard Kippenberg has pointed this out on a number of occasions in recent years. See Kippenberg, "Europe: Arena of Pluralisation and Diversification of Religions," *Journal of Religion in Europe* 1 (2008): 133–55.

6. See the wonderful book by Michael Borgolte, *Juden, Christen, Muselmanen. Die Erben der Antike und der Aufstieg des Abendlandes 300–1400 n. Chr.* (Munich: Siedler, 2006).

7. Philip Jenkins, *The Lost History of Christianity: The Thousand-Year Golden Age of the Church in the Middle East, Africa and Asia* (Oxford: Lion, 2008).

8. For an overview, see José Casanova, "The Religious Situation in Europe," in *Secularization*, ed. Joas and Wiegandt, 206–28; Andrew Greeley, *Religion in Europe at the End of the Second Millennium* (New Brunswick, NJ: Transaction, 2003); Bertelsmann Stiftung, ed., *What the World Believes*; Philip Jenkins, *God's Continent: Christianity, Islam, and Europe's Religious Crisis* (Oxford: Oxford University Press, 2007).

9. Ute Schneider, "Von Juden und Türken. Zum gegenwärtigen Diskurs über Religion, kollektive Identität und Modernisierung," *Zeitschrift für Geschichtswissenschaft* 52 (2004): 426–40, refutes such arguments very well.

10. See Joas and Wiegandt, eds., *Cultural Values of Europe*; for my introduction, see 1–21.

Bibliography

Angenendt, Arnold. *Toleranz und Gewalt. Das Christentum zwischen Bibel und Schwert*. Münster: Aschendorff, 2008.

Appleby, R. Scott. *The Ambivalence of the Sacred. Religion, Violence, and Reconciliation*. Oxford: Rowman and Littlefield, 2000.

Assmann, Jan. *The Price of Monotheism*. Stanford, CA: Stanford University Press, 2009.

Bäckström, Anders, and Grace Davie. "A Preliminary Conclusion: Gathering the Threads and Moving on." In *Welfare and Religion in 21st Century Europe*, vol. 1: *Configuring the Connections*, ed. Anders Bäckström and Grace Davie, 183–97. Burlington, VT: Ashgate, 2010.

Baily, C. A. *The Birth of the Modern World, 1780–1914*. Oxford: Blackwell, 2004.

Banfield, Edward. *The Moral Basis of a Backward Society*. New York: Free Press, 1958.

Beck, Ulrich. *Risk Society: Towards a New Modernity*. Newbury Park, CA: Sage, 1992.

Beck, Ulrich. *A God of One's Own: Religion's Capacity for Peace and Potential for Violence*. Cambridge: Polity Press, 2010.

Bedford-Strohm, Heinrich. *Gemeinschaft aus kommunikativer Freiheit*. Gütersloh: Gütersloher Verlagshaus, 1999.

Bediako, Kwame. *Christianity in Africa: The Renewal of a Non-Western Religion*. Maryknoll, NY: Orbis Books, 1995.

Bell, Daniel. "The Return of the Sacred?" In id., *The Winding Passage. Essays and Sociological Journeys, 1960–1980*, 324–54. Cambridge, MA: Abt Books, 1980.

Bellah, Robert N. *Tokugawa Religion: The Cultural Roots of Modern Japan*. New York: Free Press, 1957.

———. "What is Axial about the Axial Age?" *European Journal of Sociology* 46 (2005): 69–90.

———. "Religious Pluralism and Religious Truth." In *The Robert Bellah Reader*, ed. Robert N. Bellah and Steve Tipton, 474–89. Durham, NC: Duke University Press, 2006.

————. *Religion in Human Evolution.* Cambridge, MA: Belknap Press of Harvard University Press, 2011.

Bellah, Robert N., et al. *Habits of the Heart: Individualism and Commitment in American Life.* Berkeley, CA: University of California Press, 1985.

Bellah, Robert N., and Hans Joas, eds. *The Axial Age and Its Consequences.* Cambridge, MA: Belknap Press of Harvard University Press, 2012.

Bender, Thomas. *Community and Social Change in America.* New Brunswick, NJ: Rutgers University Press, 1978.

Berger, Peter L. *A Far Glory: The Quest for Faith in an Age of Credulity.* New York: Free Press, 1992.

Berger, Peter L. "Protestantism and the Quest for Certainty." *Christian Century,* August 26–September 2 (1998): 782–96.

Bertelsmann Stiftung, ed. *What the World Believes: Analyses and Commentary on the Religion Monitor 2008.* Gütersloh: Bertelsmann, 2009.

Blaschke, Olaf. "Das 19. Jahrhundert. Ein zweites konfessionelles Zeitalter?" *Geschichte und Gesellschaft* 26 (2000): 38–75.

Böckenförde, Ernst-Wolfgang. "Das unselige Handeln nach Kirchenraison." *Süddeutsche Zeitung,* April 29, 2010, 2.

Borgolte, Michael. *Juden, Christen, Muselmanen. Die Erben der Antike und der Aufstieg des Abendlandes 300–1400 n. Chr.* Munich: Siedler, 2006.

Borutta, Manuel. *Antikatholizismus. Deutschland und Italien im Zeitalter der Kulturkämpfe.* Göttingen: Vandenhoeck & Ruprecht, 2010.

Borutta, Manuel. "Genealogie der Säkularisierungstheorie. Zur Historisierung einer großen Erzählung der Moderne." *Geschichte und Gesellschaft* 36 (2010): 347–76.

Brague, Rémi. "Schluß mit den 'drei Monotheismen'!" *Communio* 2 (2007): 98–113.

Braungart, Wolfgang. "Subjekt Europa, Europas Subjekt. Novalis' katholische Provokation. Die Christenheit oder Europa." *Sinn und Form* 63 (2011): 542–58.

Brown, Callum. *The Death of Christian Britain: Understanding Secularisation, 1800–2000.* London: Routledge, 2001.

Bruce, Steve. *Secularization: In Defence of an Unfashionable Theory.* Oxford: Oxford University Press, 2011.

Brusco, Elizabeth. *The Reformation of Machismo.* Austin: University of Texas Press, 1995.

Burckhardt, Jacob. *Reflections on History.* 1905 (written 1868). London: Allen & Unwin, 1943.

Burgess, E. W. *The Family: From Institution to Companionship.* New York: American Book Co., 1945.

Carroll S. J., Anthony J. *Protestant Modernity. Weber, Secularisation and Protestantism.* Scranton, PA: University of Scranton Press, 2007.

Casanova, José. *Public Religions in the Modern World.* Chicago: University of Chicago Press, 1994.

Casanova, José. "The Religious Situation in Europe." In *Secularization and the World Religions,* ed. Hans Joas and Klaus Wiegandt, 206–28. Liverpool: Liverpool University Press, 2009.

Casanova, José. *Europas Angst vor der Religion.* Berlin: Berlin University Press, 2009.

Chadwick, Owen. *The Secularization of the European Mind in the 19th Century.* Cambridge: Cambridge University Press, 1975.

Christiano, Kevin. "Clio Goes to Church. Revisiting and Revitalizing Historical Thinking in the Sociology of Religion." *Sociology of Religion* 69 (2008): 1–28.

Collins, Randall. *Macrohistory: Essays in Sociology of the Long Run.* Stanford, CA: Stanford University Press, 1999.

Conze, Werner, Hans Wolfgang Strätz and Hermann Zabel. "Säkularisation, Säkularisierung." In *Geschichtliche Grundbegriffe,* vol. 5, ed. Otto Brunner, Werner Conze, and Reinhart Koselleck, 789–829. Stuttgart: Klett-Cotta, 1984.

Davie, Grace. *Religion in Modern Europe. A Memory Mutates.* Oxford: Oxford University Press, 2000.

Deschner, Karlheinz. *Kriminalgeschichte des Christentums.* 10 vols. Reinbek: Rowohlt, 1986–2013.

Dewey, John. *The Quest for Certainty.* London: Allen & Unwin, 1929.

Dobbelaere, Karel. *Secularization: An Analysis at Three Levels.* Brussels: Peter Lang, 2002.

Dreier, Horst. "Kanonistik und Konfessionalisierung—Marksteine auf dem Weg zum Staat." In *Artibus ingenuis,* ed. Georg Siebeck, 133–69. Tübingen: Mohr, 2001.

Durkheim, Emile. *The Division of Labour in Society.* 1893. Basingstoke, UK: Macmillan, 1984.

Durkheim, Emile. *The Elementary Forms of the Religious Life.* 1912. Oxford: Oxford University Press, 2001.

Eisenstadt, Shmuel. "The Axial Age in World History." In *The Cultural Values of Europe,* ed. Hans Joas and Klaus Wiegandt, 22–42. Liverpool: Liverpool University Press, 2008.

Fielding, Henry. *Joseph Andrew's Abenteuer.* Berlin: Aufbau, 1974.

Finke, Roger, and Rodney Stark. *The Churching of America, 1776–1990.* New Brunswick, NJ: Rutgers University Press, 1992.

Foner, Nancy, and Richard Alba. "Immigrant Religion in the U.S. and Western Europe: Bridge or Barrier to Inclusion?" *International Migration Review* 42 (2008): 360–92.

Friedrich II, king of Prussia. *Die Politischen Testamente.* Berlin: Hobbing, 1922.

Gauchet, Marcel. *La révolution des droits de l'homme*. Paris: Gallimard, 1989.

Gentz, Joachim. "The Religious Situation in East Asia." In *Secularization and the World Religions*, ed. Hans Joas and Klaus Wiegandt, 241–77. Liverpool: Liverpool University Press, 2009.

Geyer, Michael and Charles Bright. "Global Violence and Nationalizing Wars in Eurasia and America. The Geopolitics of War in the Mid Nineteenth-Century." *Comparative Studies in Society and History* 38 (1996): 619–57.

Girard, René. *Violence and the Sacred*. Baltimore, MD: Johns Hopkins University Press, 1977.

Gorski, Philip S. *The Disciplinary Revolution: Calvinism and the Rise of the State in Early Modern Europe*. Chicago: University of Chicago Press, 2003.

Graf, Friedrich Wilhelm. "Kulturprotestantismus. Zur Begriffsgeschichte einer theologiepolitischen Chiffre." In *Kulturprotestantismus. Beiträge zu einer Gestalt des modernen Christentums*, ed. Hans Martin Müller, 21–77. Gütersloh: Mohn, 1992.

Graf, Friedrich Wilhelm. "Protestantism." In *Secularization and the World Religions*, ed. Hans Joas and Klaus Wiegandt, 46–76. Liverpool: Liverpool University Press, 2007.

Greeley, Andrew. "Protestant and Catholic. Is the Analogical Imagination Extinct?" *American Sociological Review* 54 (1989): 485–502.

Greeley, Andrew. *Religion in Europe at the End of the Second Millennium*. New Brunswick, NJ: Transaction, 2003.

Grimm, Brian J., and Roger Finke. "Religious Persecution in Cross-National Context: Clashing Civilizations or Regulated Religious Economies?" *American Sociological Review* 72 (2007): 633–58.

Gross, Peter. *Die Multioptionsgesellschaft*. Frankfurt am Main: Suhrkamp, 1994.

Gross, Peter. *Jenseits der Erlösung. Die Wiederkehr der Religion und die Zukunft des Christentums*. Bielefeld: Transcript, 2007.

Hasenclever, Andreas. "Getting Religion Right. Zur Rolle von Religionen in politischen Konflikten. " In *Religion und globale Entwicklung*, ed. Jürgen Willhelm and Hartmut Ihne, 170–86. Berlin: Berlin University Press, 2009.

Heitmeyer, Wilhelm. "Das Desintegrationstheorem. Ein Erklärungsansatz zu fremdenfeindlich motivierter rechtsextremistischer Gewalt und zur Lähmung gesellschaftlicher Institutionen." In *Das Gewaltdilemma*, ed. Wilhelm Heitmeyer, 29–72. Frankfurt am Main: Suhrkamp, 1994.

Hénaff, Marcel. *The Price of Truth: Gift, Money, and Philosophy*. Stanford, CA: Stanford University Press, 2010.

Hintze, Otto. *Die Hohenzollern und ihr Werk*. Berlin: Parey, 1915.

Hirschman, Albert. *The Passions and the Interests: Political Arguments for Capitalism before Its Triumph*. Princeton, NJ: Princeton University Press, 1977.

Hobsbawm, Eric. *The Age of Capital, 1848–1875.* London: Weidenfeld & Nicolson, 1975.

Hölscher, Lucian. "Die Religion des Bürgers. Bürgerliche Frömmigkeit und protestantische Kirche im 19. Jahrhundert." *Historische Zeitschrift* 250 (1990): 595–629.

Hook, Sidney. *Reason, Social Myths and Democracy.* New York: John Day, 1940.

Huber, Wolfgang. "The Judeo-Christian Tradition." In *The Cultural Values of Europe,* ed. Hans Joas and Klaus Wiegandt, 43–59. Liverpool: Liverpool University Press, 2008.

Huber, Wolfgang. "Religion, Politik und Gewalt in der heutigen Welt." In *Weltreligionen. Verstehen, Verständigung, Verantwortung,* ed. Karl Kardinal Lehmann, 232–51. Frankfurt am Main: Verlag der Weltreligionen, 2009.

Huntington, Samuel. *The Clash of Civilizations?* Washington, DC: American Enterprise Institute, 1992.

James, William. *The Will to Believe.* 1896. London: Longmans, 1905.

James, William. *The Varieties of Religious Experience.* 1902. Cambridge, MA: Harvard University Press, 1985.

Jaspers, Karl. *The Origin and Goal of History.* 1949; English trans., 1953. London: Routledge, 2011.

Jellinek, Georg. *Die Erklärung der Menschen- und Bürgerrechte: Ein Beitrag zur modernen Verfassungsgeschichte.* Leipzig: Duncker & Humblot, 1895. Translated as *The Declarations of the Rights of Man and of Citizens: A Contribution to Modern Constitutional History* (New York: Holt, 1901).

Jenkins, Philip. *The Next Christendom: The Coming of Global Christianity.* Oxford: Oxford University Press, 2004.

Jenkins, Philip. *God's Continent: Christianity, Islam, and Europe's Religious Crisis.* Oxford: Oxford University Press, 2007.

Jenkins, Philip. *The Lost History of Christianity: The Thousand-Year Golden Age of the Church in the Middle East, Africa and Asia.* Oxford: Lion, 2008.

Joas, Hans. "Das Risiko der Gegenwartsdiagnose." *Soziologische Revue* 11 (1988): 1–6.

———. *The Creativity of Action.* Chicago: University of Chicago Press, 1996.

———. "Globalisierung und Wertentstehung—Oder: Warum Marx und Engels doch nicht recht hatten." *Berliner Journal für Soziologie* 8 (1998): 329–32.

———. *The Genesis of Values.* Chicago: University of Chicago Press, 2000.

———. "The Gift of Life. Parsons' Late Sociology of Religion," *Journal of Classical Sociology 1* (2001), 127–41

———. *War and Modernity.* Cambridge: Polity Press, 2003.

———. "Kontingenzbewußtsein. Der erste Weltkrieg und der Bruch im Zeitbewußtsein der Moderne." In *Aggression und Katharsis. Der Erste Weltkrieg im Diskurs der Moderne,* ed. Petra Ernst et al., 43–56. Vienna: Passagen, 2004.

————. "Max Weber and the Origins of Human Rights." In *Max Weber's Economy and Society: A Critical Companion*, ed. Charles Camic, Philip Gorski, and David Trubek, 366–82. Stanford, CA: Stanford University Press, 2005.

————. *Do We Need Religion? On the Experience of Self-Transcendence*. Boulder, CO: Paradigm, 2007.

————. "Ohne einen Finger zu krümmen, sind wir erlöst." *Frankfurter Allgemeine Zeitung*, May 5, 2008, 41.

————. "Society, State and Religion: Their Relationship from the Perspective of the World Religions." In *Secularization and the World Religions*, ed. Hans Joas and Klaus Wiegandt, 1–22. Liverpool: Liverpool University Press, 2009.

————. "The Religious Situation in the U.S.A." In *Secularization and the World Religions*, ed. Hans Joas and Klaus Wiegandt, 229–40. Liverpool: Liverpool University Press, 2009.

————. "Die säkulare Option. Ihr Aufstieg und ihre Folgen." *Deutsche Zeitschrift für Philosophie* 57 (2009): 293–300.

————. "The Religious Situation in the United States." In *What the World Believes: Analyses and Commentary on the Religion Monitor 2008*, ed. Bertelsmann-Stiftung, 317–34. Gütersloh: Bertelsmann, 2009.

————. "Die Selbständigkeit religiöser Phänomene. Ernst Troeltsch als Vorbild der Religionsforschung." *Fuge. Journal für Religion und Moderne* 6 (2010): 15–28.

————. "Review of Anthony J. Carroll S. J., Protestant Modernity." *Journal of Religion* 90 (2010): 445–47.

————. "The Contingency of Secularization. Reflections on the Problem of Secularization in the Work of Reinhart Koselleck." In *The Benefit of Broad Horizons. Intellectual and Institutional Preconditions for a Global Social Science. Festschrift for Björn Wittrock*, ed. Hans Joas and Barbro Klein, 87–104. Leiden: Brill, 2010.

————. "The Axial Age Debate as Religious Discourse." In *The Axial Age and Its Consequences*, ed. Robert N. Bellah and Hans Joas, 9–29. Cambridge, MA: Belknap Press of Harvard University Press, 2012.

————. "Gefährliche Prozeßbegriffe. Eine Warnung vor der Rede von Differenzierung, Rationalisierung und Modernisierung." In *Umstrittene Säkularisierung. Soziologische und historische Analysen zur Differenzierung von Religion und Politik*, ed. Karl Gabriel et al., 603–22. Berlin: Berlin University Press, 2012.

————. "Peace through Democracy?" *European Journal of Social Theory* 15 (2012): 21–34.

————. *The Sacredness of the Person: A New Genealogy of Human Rights*. Washington, DC: Georgetown University Press, 2013.

Joas, Hans, and Frank Adloff. "Transformations of German Civil Society: Milieu

Change and Community Spirit." In *Civil Society: Berlin Perspectives*, ed. John Keane, 103–38. New York: Berghahn, 2006.

Joas, Hans, and Wolfgang Knöbl. *Social Theory: Twenty Introductory Lectures.* Cambridge: Cambridge University Press, 2009.

———. *War in Social Thought: Hobbes to the Present.* Princeton, NJ: Princeton University Press, 2012.

———, eds. *Gewalt in den USA.* Frankfurt am Main: Fischer, 1994.

Joas, Hans, and Klaus Wiegandt, eds. *The Cultural Values of Europe.* Liverpool: Liverpool University Press, 2008.

———, eds. *Secularization and the World Religions.* Liverpool: Liverpool University Press, 2009.

Johnson, Ian. "China Gets Religion!" *New York Review of Books*, December 22, 2011, 55–8.

Jung, Matthias. *Der bewußte Ausdruck. Anthropologie der Artikulation.* Berlin: De Gruyter, 2009.

Kane, Daniella, and Jung Mee Park. "The Puzzle of Korean Christianity: Geopolitical Networks and Religious Conversion in Early Twentieth-Century East Asia." *American Journal of Sociology* 115 (2009): 365–404.

Kaufmann, Franz-Xaver. "Zwischenräume und Wechselwirkungen. Der Verlust der Zentralperspektive und das Christentum." *Theologie und Glaube* 96 (2006): 309–23.

———. *Kirchenkrise. Wie überlebt das Christentum?* Freiburg: Herder, 2011.

Kippenberg, Hans Gerhard. "Europe: Arena of Pluralisation and Diversification of Religions." *Journal of Religion in Europe* 1 (2008): 133–55.

———. *Violence as Worship. Religious Wars in the Age of Globalization.* Stanford, CA: Stanford University Press, 2011.

———. "Zur Kontingenz religiösen Gewalthandelns." In *Handlung und Erfahrung. Das Erbe von Historismus und Pragmatismus und die Zukunft der Sozialtheorie*, ed. Bettina Hollstein et al., 191–216. Frankfurt am Main: Campus, 2011.

Kippenberg, Hans Gerhard, and Kocku von Stuckrad. *Einführung in die Religionswissenschaft.* Munich: Beck, 2003.

Knöbl, Wolfgang. *Spielräume der Modernisierung. Das Ende der Eindeutigkeit.* Weilerswist: Velbrück, 2001.

Kohlberg, Lawrence. "Stage and Sequence: The Cognitive-Developmental Approach to Socialization" In *Handbook of Socialization Theory and Research*, ed. David A. Goslin, 347–480. Chicago: Rand McNally, 1969.

Koselleck, Reinhart. *Critique and Crisis. Enlightenment and the Pathogenesis of Modern Society.* Cambridge, MA: MIT Press, 1988.

Krakau, Knud. *Missionsbewusstsein und Völkerrechtsdoktrin in den Vereinigten Staaten von Amerika.* Frankfurt am Main: Metzner, 1967.

Krakau, Knud. "American Foreign Relations: A National Style?" *Diplomatic History* 8 (1984): 253–72.

Lehmann, Cardinal Karl. "Catholic Christianity." In *Secularization and the World Religions*, ed. Hans Joas and Klaus Wiegandt, 23–45. Liverpool: Liverpool University Press, 2009.

Lehmann, Karsten. "Community-Kirchen im Wandel. Zur Entwicklung christlicher Migrantengemeinden zwischen 1950 und 2000." *Berliner Journal für Soziologie* 16 (2006): 485–501.

Lepsius, Rainer. "Parteiensystem und Sozialstruktur. Zum Problem der Demokratisierung der deutschen Gesellschaft." 1966. Reprinted in id., *Demokratie in Deutschland*, 25–50. Göttingen: Vandenhoeck & Ruprecht, 1993.

Leskov, Nikolai. *On the Edge of the World.* Crestwood, N.Y.: St. Vladimir's Seminary Press, 1993.

Lübbe, Hermann. *Säkularisierung. Geschichte eines ideenpolitischen Begriffs.* Freiburg: Karl Alber, 1965.

Luckmann, Thomas. *The Invisible Religion: The Problem of Religion in Modern Society.* New York: Macmillan, 1967.

Lyotard, Jean-François. *The Postmodern Condition: A Report on Knowledge.* Minneapolis: University of Minnesota Press, 1984.

Malinowski, Bronislaw. *Crime and Custom in Savage Society.* London: Kegan Paul, 1926.

Markschies, Christoph. *Warum hat das Christentum in der Antike überlebt? Ein Beitrag zum Gespräch zwischen Kirchengeschichte und Systematischer Theologie.* Forum Theologische Literaturzeitung. Leipzig: Evangelische Verlagsanstalt, 2004.

Marramao, Giacomo. *Die Säkularisierung der westlichen Welt.* Frankfurt am Main: Insel, 1996.

Martin, David. "Towards Eliminating the Concept of Secularization." In *Penguin Survey of the Social Sciences*, ed. Julius Gould, 169–82. London: Penguin Books, 1965.

———. *A General Theory of Secularization.* Oxford: Blackwell, 1978.

———. *On Secularization. Towards a Revised General Theory.* Burlington, VT: Ashgate, 2005.

———. "Secularisation and the Future of Christianity." *Journal of Contemporary Religion* 20 (2005): 145–60.

———. "The Relevance of the European Model of Secularization in Latin America and Africa." In *Secularization and the World Religions*, ed. Hans Joas and Klaus Wiegandt, 278–95. Liverpool: Liverpool University Press, 2009.

———. *The Future of Christianity: Reflections on Violence and Democracy, Religion and Secularization.* Burlington, VT: Ashgate, 2011.

———. "Pentecostalism: Transnational Voluntarism in the Global Religious

Economy." In id., *The Future of Christianity. Reflections on Violence and Democracy, Religion and Secularization*, 63–84. Burlington, VT: Ashgate, 2011.

Marx, Karl. *Critique of Hegel's Philosophy of Right*. Cambridge: CUP Archive, 1977.

Mauss, Marcel. *The Gift*. 1923. London: Routledge, 2002.

McLeod, Hugh. *Piety and Poverty: Working-Class Religion in Berlin, London and New York, 1870–1914*. New York: Holmes & Meier, 1996.

———. *Religion and the People of Western Europe, 1789–1989*. Oxford: Oxford University Press, 1997.

———. *Secularization in Western Europe, 1848–1914*. New York: St Martin's Press, 2000.

———. *The Religious Crisis of the 1960s*. Oxford: Oxford University Press, 2007.

Merton, Robert K. "Puritanism, Pietism, and Science." *Sociological Review* 28 (1936): 1–30.

———. *Science, Technology and Society in Seventeenth-Century England*. 1938. New York: Howard Fertig, 1970.

Mitchell, Joshua. "Religion Is Not a Preference." *Journal of Politics* 69 (2007): 351–62.

Myers, Gerald. *William James: His Life and Thought*. New Haven, CT: Yale University Press, 1986.

Neem, Johann N. "The Early Republic: Thomas Jefferson's Philosophy of History and the Future of American Christianity." In *Prophesies of Godlessness: Predictions of America's Imminent Secularization from the Puritans to the Present Day*, ed. Charles Mathewes and Christopher McKnight Nichols, 35–52. Oxford: Oxford University Press, 2008.

Nipperdey, Thomas. *Deutsche Geschichte, 1800–1918*. 3 vols. Munich: Beck, 1983–92.

Norris, Pippa, and Ronald Inglehart. *Sacred and Secular: Religion and Politics Worldwide*. Cambridge: Cambridge University Press, 2004.

Novalis [Georg Philipp Friedrich von Hardenberg]. "Christianity or Europe: A Fragment." 1799. In *The Early Political Writings of the German Romantics*, ed. Frederick C. Beiser, 59–80. Cambridge: Cambridge University Press, 1996.

O'Malley, John. *Trent and All That: Renaming Catholicism in the Early Modern Era*. Cambridge, MA: Harvard University Press, 2000.

Osterhammel, Jürgen. *Die Verwandlung der Welt. Eine Geschichte des 19. Jahrhunderts*. Munich: Beck, 2009.

Otto, Rudolf. *The Idea of the Holy*. 1917. Oxford: Oxford University Press, 1950.

Padover, Saul, ed. *The Complete Jefferson*. New York: Duell, Sloan & Pearce, 1943.

Parsons, Talcott. "Comparative Studies and Evolutionary Change." In id., *Social Systems and the Evolution of Action Theory*, 279–320. New York: Free Press, 1977.

———. "Christianity." In id., *Action Theory and the Human Condition*, 73–212. New York: Free Press, 1978.

———. "Religion in Postindustrial America." In id., *Action Theory and the Human Condition*, 300–22. New York: Free Press, 1978.

Paul, Gregory. "Cross-National Correlations of Quantifiable Societal Health with Popular Religiosity and Secularism in the Prosperous Democracies." *Journal of Religion and Society* 7 (2005): 1–17.

Perry, Ralph Barton. *Puritanism and Democracy.* New York: Vanguard, 1944.

Pew Forum on Religion and Public Life. *U.S. Religious Landscape Survey 2009.* Washington, D.C.: Pew Forum, 2009.

Piaget, Jean. *The Moral Judgement of the Child.* 1932. Harmondsworth, UK: Penguin Books, 1977.

Pollack, Detlef. *Säkularisierung—ein moderner Mythos?* Tübingen: Mohr, 2003.

Putnam, Robert, and David Campbell. *American Grace: How Religion Divides and Unites Us.* New York: Simon & Schuster, 2010.

Reinhard, Marcel. *Paris pendant la Révolution.* 2 vols. Paris: Centre de documentation universitaire, 1966.

Reinhard, Wolfgang. "'Modernisierung' und Modernisierung. Erfahrungen mit dem Konzept 'Modernisierung' in der neueren Geschichte." In *Innovation und Originalität*, ed. Walter Haug and Burghart Wachinger, 53–69. Tübingen: Niemeyer, 1993.

———. *Lebensformen Europas. Eine historische Kulturanthropologie.* Munich: Beck, 2004.

Ricœur, Paul. "Love and Justice." In id., *Figuring the Sacred: Religion, Narrative and Imagination*, 315–29. Minneapolis, MN: Fortress Press, 1995.

Rorty, Richard. "Failed Prophecies, Glorious Hopes." In id., *Philosophy and Social Hope*, 202–9. London: Penguin Books, 1999.

Runciman, W. G. "The Diffusion of Christianity in the Third Century AD as a Case-Study in the Theory of Cultural Selection." *European Journal of Sociology* 45 (2004): 3–21.

Sahlins, Marshall. *Stone Age Economics.* New York: Aldine de Gruyter, 1972.

Santayana, George. "Reason in Religion." In id., *Works*, 4: 3–206. New York: Scribner's, 1936.

Scheler, Max. *On the Eternal in Man.* 1923. New Brunswick, NJ: Transaction, 2010.

Scheler, Max. "Man in an Era of Adjustment." 1927. In id., *Philosophical Perspectives*, 94–126. Boston: Beacon Press, 1958.

Schieder, Rolf. *Sind Religionen gefährlich?* Berlin: Berlin University Press, 2008.

Schmitt, Carl. *Roman Catholicism and Political Form.* 1923. Westport, CT: Greenwood Press, 1996.

Schnabel, Franz. *Deutsche Geschichte im neunzehnten Jahrhundert.* Vol. 4: *Die religiösen Kräfte.* 1937. Munich: DTV, 1987.

Schneider, Ute. "Von Juden und Türken. Zum gegenwärtigen Diskurs über Religion, kollektive Identität und Modernisierung." *Zeitschrift für Geschichtswissenschaft* 52 (2004): 426–40.

Schulze, Gerhard. *Die Erlebnisgesellschaft. Kultursoziologie der Gegenwart.* Frankfurt am Main: Campus, 1992.

Senghaas, Dieter. "The Realities of Cultural Struggles." In *The Cultural Values of Europe*, ed. Hans Joas and Klaus Wiegandt, 320–37. Liverpool: Liverpool University Press, 2008.

Sennett, Richard. *The Corrosion of Character: The Personal Consequences of Work in the New Capitalism.* New York: Norton, 1998.

Shin, Jin-Wook. *Modernisierung und Zivilgesellschaft in Südkorea.* Berlin: Deutscher Universitätsverlag, 2005.

Silver, Daniel. "Religion without Instrumentalization." *Archives européennes de sociologie* 47 (2006): 421–34.

Sinnott-Armstrong, Walter. *Morality without God?* Oxford: Oxford University Press, 2009.

Smith, Christian: "Introduction: Rethinking the Secularization of American Public Life." In id., ed., *The Secular Revolution: Power, Interests, and Conflict in the Secularization of American Public Life*, 1–96. Berkeley, CA: University of California Press, 2003.

Spilka, Bernhard, et al. *The Psychology of Religion: An Empirical Approach.* 4th ed. New York: Guilford Press, 2009.

Stark, Rodney. "Secularization, R.I.P." *Sociology of Religion* 60 (1999): 249–73.

Sterne, Lawrence. *The Life and Opinions of Tristram Shandy, Gentleman.* 1759–67. Edited by Melvyn New and Joan New. 2 vols. Gainesville: University Presses of Florida, 1978.

Tackett, Timothy. "The French Revolution and Religion to 1794." In *Enlightenment, Reawakening and Revolution, 1660–1815*, Cambridge History of Christianity, vol. 7, ed. Stewart J. Brown and Timothy Tackett, 536–55. Cambridge: Cambridge University Press, 2006.

Taylor, Charles. *Sources of the Self: The Making of the Modern Identity.* Cambridge, MA: Harvard University Press, 1989.

———. *A Secular Age.* Cambridge MA: Belknap Press of Harvard University Press, 2007.

———. "The Polysemy of the Secular." *Social Research* 76, no. 4 (2009): 1143–66.

Tocqueville, Alexis de. *The Ancien Régime and the Revolution.* 1856. London: Penguin Books, 2008.

Toulmin, Stephen. *Cosmopolis: The Hidden Agenda of Modernity.* New York: Free Press, 1990.

Troeltsch, Ernst. "Atheistische Ethik." 1895. In id., *Gesammelte Schriften*, 2: 525–55. Tübingen: Mohr, 1912.

————. "Political Ethics and Christianity." 1904. In id., *Religion in History*, 173–209. Minneapolis, MN: Fortress Press, 1997.

————. "Das Wesen des modernen Geistes." 1907. In id., *Aufsätze zur Geistesgeschichte und Religionssoziologie*, 297–338. Tübingen: Mohr, 1925.

————. "Die Bedeutung des Begriffs der Kontingenz." 1910. In id., *Gesammelte Schriften*, 2: 769–78. Tübingen: Mohr, 1922.

————. "Die Zukunftsmöglichkeiten des Christentums." *Logos* 1 (1910–11): 165–85.

————. *Die Soziallehren der christlichen Kirchen und Gruppen* (Tübingen, 1912). Trans. as *The Social Teaching of the Christian Churches* (1931).

————. *Kritische Gesamtausgabe*. Vol. 8: *Schriften zur Bedeutung des Protestantismus für die moderne Welt, 1906–1913*. Berlin: De Gruyter, 2001.

————. "Das Verhältnis des Protestantismus zur Kultur. Überblick." In id., *Gesammelte Schriften*, 4: 191–202. Tübingen: Mohr, 1925.

Voegelin, Eric. *Political Religions*. 1938. Lewiston, NY: E. Mellen, 1985.

Vogt, Peter. *Kontingenz und Zufall. Eine Ideen- und Begriffsgeschichte*. Berlin: Akademie, 2011.

Weber, Marianne. *Max Weber: A Biography*. New York: Wiley, 1975.

Weber, Max. *The Protestant Ethic and the Spirit of Capitalism*. 1904. New York: Oxford University Press, 2011.

————. *Economy and Society*. Berkeley: University of California Press, 1979.

Wilcox, Clyde, et al. "Religious Preferences and Social Science: A Second Look." *Journal of Politics* 69 (2007): 874–79.

Wolf, Christof. "Religiöse Sozialisation, konfessionelle Milieus und Generation." *Zeitschrift für Soziologie* 24 (1995): 345–57.

Wuthnow, Robert. *The Restructuring of American Religion*. Princeton, NJ: Princeton University Press, 1988.

Yack, Bernard, *The Fetishism of Modernities: Epochal Self-Consciousness in Contemporary Social and Political Thought*. Notre Dame, IN: University of Notre Dame Press, 1997.

Zuckerman, Phil. *Society without God: What the Least Religious Nations Can Tell Us About Contentment*. New York: New York University Press, 2008.

Acknowledgments of Prior Publication

Although substantially expanded and revised, the following chapters of this book are based on previously published essays:

Parts of chapter 1 appear in Hans Joas and Alan Wolfe, *Beyond the Separation between Church and State? WRR Lecture 2006,* ed. Wetenschappelijke Raad voor het Regeringsbeleid (Scientific Council for Government Policy), 15–26 (The Hague: WRR, 2006).

Parts of chapter 6 appear in Hans Joas, "Morality in the Age of Contingency." *Acta Sociologica* 47 (2004): 392–99.

Parts of chapter 7 appear in Wolfram Weisse et al., eds., *Religions and Dialogue: International Approaches* (Münster: Waxmann, 2014), 33–40.

Chapter 9: Hans Joas, "The Future of Christianity," *Hedgehog Review* 13 (2011): 74–82.

Index

Cultural Memory in the Present

Jean-François Lyotard, *Enthusiasm: The Kantian Critique of History*

Ernst van Alphen, Mieke Bal, and Carel Smith, eds., *The Rhetoric of Sincerity*

Stéphane Mosès, *The Angel of History: Rosenzweig, Benjamin, Scholem*

Pierre Hadot, *The Present Alone Is Our Happiness: Conversations with Jeannie Carlier and Arnold I. Davidson*

Alexandre Lefebvre, *The Image of the Law: Deleuze, Bergson, Spinoza*

Samira Haj, *Reconfiguring Islamic Tradition: Reform, Rationality, and Modernity*

Diane Perpich, *The Ethics of Emmanuel Levinas*

Marcel Detienne, *Comparing the Incomparable*

François Delaporte, *Anatomy of the Passions*

René Girard, *Mimesis and Theory: Essays on Literature and Criticism, 1959–2005*

Richard Baxstrom, *Houses in Motion: The Experience of Place and the Problem of Belief in Urban Malaysia*

Jennifer L. Culbert, *Dead Certainty: The Death Penalty and the Problem of Judgment*

Samantha Frost, *Lessons from a Materialist Thinker: Hobbesian Reflections on Ethics and Politics*

Regina Mara Schwartz, *Sacramental Poetics at the Dawn of Secularism: When God Left the World*

Gil Anidjar, *Semites: Race, Religion, Literature*

Ranjana Khanna, *Algeria Cuts: Women and Representation, 1830 to the Present*

Esther Peeren, *Intersubjectivities and Popular Culture: Bakhtin and Beyond*

Eyal Peretz, *Becoming Visionary: Brian De Palma's Cinematic Education of the Senses*

Diana Sorensen, *A Turbulent Decade Remembered: Scenes from the Latin American Sixties*

Hubert Damisch, *A Childhood Memory by Piero della Francesca*

José van Dijck, *Mediated Memories in the Digital Age*

Dana Hollander, *Exemplarity and Chosenness: Rosenzweig and Derrida on the Nation of Philosophy*

Asja Szafraniec, *Beckett, Derrida, and the Event of Literature*

Sara Guyer, *Romanticism After Auschwitz*

Alison Ross, *The Aesthetic Paths of Philosophy: Presentation in Kant, Heidegger, Lacoue-Labarthe, and Nancy*

Gerhard Richter, *Thought-Images: Frankfurt School Writers' Reflections from Damaged Life*

Bella Brodzki, *Can These Bones Live? Translation, Survival, and Cultural Memory*

Rodolphe Gasché, *The Honor of Thinking: Critique, Theory, Philosophy*

Brigitte Peucker, *The Material Image: Art and the Real in Film*

Natalie Melas, *All the Difference in the World: Postcoloniality and the Ends of Comparison*

Jonathan Culler, *The Literary in Theory*

Michael G. Levine, *The Belated Witness: Literature, Testimony, and the Question of Holocaust Survival*

Jennifer A. Jordan, *Structures of Memory: Understanding German Change in Berlin and Beyond*

Christoph Menke, *Reflections of Equality*

Marlène Zarader, *The Unthought Debt: Heidegger and the Hebraic Heritage*

Jan Assmann, *Religion and Cultural Memory: Ten Studies*

David Scott and Charles Hirschkind, *Powers of the Secular Modern: Talal Asad and His Interlocutors*

Gyanendra Pandey, *Routine Violence: Nations, Fragments, Histories*

James Siegel, *Naming the Witch*

J. M. Bernstein, *Against Voluptuous Bodies: Late Modernism and the Meaning of Painting*

Theodore W. Jennings Jr., *Reading Derrida / Thinking Paul: On Justice*

Richard Rorty and Eduardo Mendieta, *Take Care of Freedom and Truth Will Take Care of Itself: Interviews with Richard Rorty*

Jacques Derrida, *Paper Machine*

Renaud Barbaras, *Desire and Distance: Introduction to a Phenomenology of Perception*

Jill Bennett, *Empathic Vision: Affect, Trauma, and Contemporary Art*

Ban Wang, *Illuminations from the Past: Trauma, Memory, and History in Modern China*

James Phillips, *Heidegger's* Volk*: Between National Socialism and Poetry*

Frank Ankersmit, *Sublime Historical Experience*

István Rév, *Retroactive Justice: Prehistory of Post-Communism*

Paola Marrati, *Genesis and Trace: Derrida Reading Husserl and Heidegger*

Krzysztof Ziarek, *The Force of Art*

Marie-José Mondzain, *Image, Icon, Economy: The Byzantine Origins of the Contemporary Imaginary*

Cecilia Sjöholm, *The Antigone Complex: Ethics and the Invention of Feminine Desire*

Jacques Derrida and Elisabeth Roudinesco, *For What Tomorrow . . . : A Dialogue*

Elisabeth Weber, *Questioning Judaism: Interviews by Elisabeth Weber*

Jacques Derrida and Catherine Malabou, *Counterpath: Traveling with Jacques Derrida*

Martin Seel, *Aesthetics of Appearing*

Nanette Salomon, *Shifting Priorities: Gender and Genre in Seventeenth-Century Dutch Painting*

Jacob Taubes, *The Political Theology of Paul*

Jean-Luc Marion, *The Crossing of the Visible*

Eric Michaud, *The Cult of Art in Nazi Germany*

Anne Freadman, *The Machinery of Talk: Charles Peirce and the Sign Hypothesis*

Stanley Cavell, *Emerson's Transcendental Etudes*

Stuart McLean, *The Event and Its Terrors: Ireland, Famine, Modernity*

Beate Rössler, ed., *Privacies: Philosophical Evaluations*

Bernard Faure, *Double Exposure: Cutting Across Buddhist and Western Discourses*

Alessia Ricciardi, *The Ends of Mourning: Psychoanalysis, Literature, Film*

Alain Badiou, *Saint Paul: The Foundation of Universalism*

Gil Anidjar, *The Jew, the Arab: A History of the Enemy*

Jonathan Culler and Kevin Lamb, eds., *Just Being Difficult? Academic Writing in the Public Arena*

Jean-Luc Nancy, *A Finite Thinking*, edited by Simon Sparks

Theodor W. Adorno, *Can One Live after Auschwitz? A Philosophical Reader*, edited by Rolf Tiedemann

Patricia Pisters, *The Matrix of Visual Culture: Working with Deleuze in Film Theory*

Andreas Huyssen, *Present Pasts: Urban Palimpsests and the Politics of Memory*

Talal Asad, *Formations of the Secular: Christianity, Islam, Modernity*

Dorothea von Mücke, *The Rise of the Fantastic Tale*

Marc Redfield, *The Politics of Aesthetics: Nationalism, Gender, Romanticism*

Emmanuel Levinas, *On Escape*

Dan Zahavi, *Husserl's Phenomenology*

Rodolphe Gasché, *The Idea of Form: Rethinking Kant's Aesthetics*

Michael Naas, *Taking on the Tradition: Jacques Derrida and the Legacies of Deconstruction*

Herlinde Pauer-Studer, ed., *Constructions of Practical Reason: Interviews on Moral and Political Philosophy*

Jean-Luc Marion, *Being Given That: Toward a Phenomenology of Givenness*

Theodor W. Adorno and Max Horkheimer, *Dialectic of Enlightenment*

Ian Balfour, *The Rhetoric of Romantic Prophecy*

Martin Stokhof, *World and Life as One: Ethics and Ontology in Wittgenstein's Early Thought*

Gianni Vattimo, *Nietzsche: An Introduction*

Jacques Derrida, *Negotiations: Interventions and Interviews, 1971–1998*, edited by Elizabeth Rottenberg

Brett Levinson, *The Ends of Literature: The Latin American "Boom" in the Neoliberal Marketplace*

Timothy J. Reiss, *Against Autonomy: Cultural Instruments, Mutualities, and the Fictive Imagination*

Hent de Vries and Samuel Weber, eds., *Religion and Media*

Niklas Luhmann, *Theories of Distinction: Re-Describing the Descriptions of Modernity*, edited and introduced by William Rasch

Johannes Fabian, *Anthropology with an Attitude: Critical Essays*

Michel Henry, *I Am the Truth: Toward a Philosophy of Christianity*

Gil Anidjar, *"Our Place in Al-Andalus": Kabbalah, Philosophy, Literature in Arab-Jewish Letters*

Hélène Cixous and Jacques Derrida, *Veils*

F. R. Ankersmit, *Historical Representation*

F. R. Ankersmit, *Political Representation*

Elissa Marder, *Dead Time: Temporal Disorders in the Wake of Modernity (Baudelaire and Flaubert)*

Reinhart Koselleck, *The Practice of Conceptual History: Timing History, Spacing Concepts*

Niklas Luhmann, *The Reality of the Mass Media*

Hubert Damisch, *A Theory of /Cloud/: Toward a History of Painting*

Jean-Luc Nancy, *The Speculative Remark: (One of Hegel's bon mots)*

Jean-François Lyotard, *Soundproof Room: Malraux's Anti-Aesthetics*

Jan Patočka, *Plato and Europe*

Hubert Damisch, *Skyline: The Narcissistic City*

Isabel Hoving, *In Praise of New Travelers: Reading Caribbean Migrant Women Writers*

Richard Rand, ed., *Futures: Of Jacques Derrida*

William Rasch, *Niklas Luhmann's Modernity: The Paradoxes of Differentiation*

Jacques Derrida and Anne Dufourmantelle, *Of Hospitality*

Jean-François Lyotard, *The Confession of Augustine*

Kaja Silverman, *World Spectators*

Samuel Weber, *Institution and Interpretation: Expanded Edition*

Jeffrey S. Librett, *The Rhetoric of Cultural Dialogue: Jews and Germans in the Epoch of Emancipation*

Ulrich Baer, *Remnants of Song: Trauma and the Experience of Modernity in Charles Baudelaire and Paul Celan*

Samuel C. Wheeler III, *Deconstruction as Analytic Philosophy*

David S. Ferris, *Silent Urns: Romanticism, Hellenism, Modernity*

Rodolphe Gasché, *Of Minimal Things: Studies on the Notion of Relation*

Sarah Winter, *Freud and the Institution of Psychoanalytic Knowledge*

Samuel Weber, *The Legend of Freud: Expanded Edition*

Aris Fioretos, ed., *The Solid Letter: Readings of Friedrich Hölderlin*

J. Hillis Miller / Manuel Asensi, *Black Holes / J. Hillis Miller; or, Boustrophedonic Reading*

Miryam Sas, *Fault Lines: Cultural Memory and Japanese Surrealism*

Peter Schwenger, *Fantasm and Fiction: On Textual Envisioning*

Didier Maleuvre, *Museum Memories: History, Technology, Art*

Jacques Derrida, *Monolingualism of the Other; or, The Prosthesis of Origin*

Andrew Baruch Wachtel, *Making a Nation, Breaking a Nation: Literature and Cultural Politics in Yugoslavia*

Niklas Luhmann, *Love as Passion: The Codification of Intimacy*

Mieke Bal, ed., *The Practice of Cultural Analysis: Exposing Interdisciplinary Interpretation*

Jacques Derrida and Gianni Vattimo, eds., *Religion*